SITE SEEING THE INTERNET
PLAIN & SIMPLE
FOR TEACHERS, PARENTS & KIDS

SITE SEEING THE INTERNET

PLAIN & SIMPLE

FOR TEACHERS, PARENTS & KIDS

Gary M. Garfield & Suzanne McDonough

PEGUIS
PUBLISHERS

WINNIPEG, MANITOBA, CANADA

Printed and bound in Canada by Friesens, Altona

96 97 98 99 00 5 4 3 2 1

Canadian Cataloguing in Publication Data

Garfield, Gary M., 1946-

   Site seeing the internet plain & simple

   ISBN 1-895411-81-5

1. Internet (Computer network) - Handbooks, manuals, etc. 2. Computer-assisted instruction. I. McDonough, Suzanne, 1959- II. Title.

TK5105.875.I57G37 1996   004.6'7   C95-920257-9

Book and Cover Design: Darlene "Toots" Toews / Lilac Studio

Peguis Publishers
100-318 McDermot Avenue
Winnipeg, Manitoba
Canada R3A 0A2

1-800-667-9673

Contents

WEB SITES 27

MOSTLY MUSEUMS 29

CYBER SCIENCE 39

PEOPLE, PLACES & PURPOSE 65

LIVELY LITERATURE 89

SITE SEEING TODAY

Site Seeing the Internet is more than a practical guide to "get you on the Internet." It is a tour of adventure, mystery, fun, and amazement. While you're on it, you'll visit hundreds of sites—from galactic outer space to the human body's inner space, from haiku to volcanoes. It's all right here, in the most magnificent tour money can't buy. And best of all, you don't need a car, ship, or plane, or a horse, bike, or train. You can do your exploring from your classroom or your own home. All you need are your computer, some imagination, and a bit of the pioneer spirit.

This book is for everyone—teachers, parents, and kids (you may, of course, fit into more than one category). It's an easy-to-use resource with clear directions and exciting places to visit. You'll tour sites where participation permits an equality of access, and go places that empower and engage you in novel pursuits unmatched by anything you've done before. You'll "walk" down the marble corridors of the Medici Palace in Florence and along the wooden floors of the Louvre in Paris; "leap" onto the surface of the moon with the astronauts; read the Dead Sea Scrolls; maybe you'll find a singalong for your four year old. Along the way, you'll find activities you can easily integrate into your curriculum (if you're a teacher) or implement on your home computer.

WHAT WE (and, of course, you) HOPE TO ACCOMPLISH

There is so much knowledge out there. Whether you access this knowledge from home or from school, we—as teachers and parents—feel we owe it to our children to introduce them to the Internet, the most significant and powerful information retrieval system of the twentieth century.

The Internet can take us on journeys of learning that until recently we could only dream about. Now that the dream has become reality, we wish to facilitate it so that all of you who wish to partake can do so.

We want to foster the excitement, the learning, and the teaching so that you, too, can experience the awe and appreciate the innovation of this powerful tool. We want to share our new-found fortune—the riches of inquiry, discovery, and information. Wherever you go on the Internet, we hope you will see the magic in the technology and the potential in the practice.

WHAT THE INTERNET IS

Imagine a huge highway system stretching from continent to continent, bridging oceans, mountains, and deserts, and extending to almost every city and town in nearly every country on earth. Along the roads are millions of places to stop—museums, libraries, stores, concert halls, movie theaters, zoos, research centers, national parks, reading rooms, universities, schools, coffee houses, the rain forest, even a coral reef. Once you're on it you can navigate wherever you wish. The roads are invisible; they may be laid out through phone lines, but more often than not, the highway stretches between two points guided by radio beams from ground to satellite, from satellite to satellite, or from satellite to ground.

All you need is a special traveling vehicle to maneuver around this network of connections, then find the "on-ramp" to begin your journey. The vehicle is your computer and the on-ramp is what is called a server or provider. Once you're on the road, a cornucopia of goodies awaits you—every day, without exception, there are hundreds of new places to visit.

HOW THE INTERNET GOT STARTED

In the mid 1960s, a communications network was established for the American government and military that would be immune to nuclear attack. The theory was, with an inter-laced computer communication system linked to servers (very, very large computers) around the United States, if one or more systems was damaged or destroyed, the remaining "linked" computers could continue to communicate. Well, that military invasion didn't occur, and the system remained intact. With tremendous advances and innovations in defense as well as in civilian communications, people realized that the many new networks (soon to be known as the Internet) could serve a new purpose. Research and development agencies and universities joined the system, and it was not long before an information revolution set in motion the urgent need for people to learn about and enter the Internet.

Anyone who was with a university, government, or the military had easy access to this system. But now, in addition to the *big* three, school children, business people, and families all want to participate in the adventure. Today, anyone with the proper equipment can access the Internet.

WHY USE THE INTERNET?

Every day, newspapers, magazines, radio, and television carry articles or stories related to the telecommunications revolution, and, more specifically, to the Internet. Even Hollywood has produced a motion picture featuring the Internet (do remember, however, that it is Hollywood). You may be interested simply because you're curious— it is the "in" conversation at schools, places of business, at home, social events, and coffee houses. Or maybe you don't want to be

stranded by the side of the road while the rest of the world is zooming
by on the information highway. Perhaps you, like many of us, enjoy
continual learning. Even some kids see the value of learning (just
don't ask them to say that in public). Finally, everyone wants to
participate in something important, and the Internet may well be the
"event" that influences who we are and where we're going. Likely, the
Internet and the information revolution will dramatically impact
humankind although the how and what of that impact remain un-
known. Pioneers take risks, but the only obvious risk here is that of
wanting more.

Whatever your reason(s) for getting on the Internet, be assured that
any anxiety you feel now will soon be followed by a calming sense of
personal confidence and understanding.

As a Teacher

For teachers, the time to teach new sets of skills and concepts is now;
it is critical that you provide your students with the skills necessary
to access the Internet. To do that, you yourself have to have the skills
to access the technology. We have crossed the threshold of how we
learn and how we view learning. It is a view of infinite resources in
which we seek through inquiry—a process that extends beyond the
knowledge of our immediate experiences. Teachers need to think
about these infinite opportunities available when encouraging
students to seek information in new ways. Learning is discovering
what we don't know, not simply reorganizing what we do.

Many educators see the Internet and the technological revolution as a
new resource, offering an expanded classroom with new ideas and
activities. With it, teachers from around the world can share with their
colleagues what they are doing. Take the time to construct a meaningful plan that will permit your students to understand this new medium
of knowledge exploration.

Integration within the curriculum is our objective when using the Internet, or any form of telecommunications or technology. Telecommunications is already part of the curriculum in many places. It is integrated into instructional units, and enhances what is being taught, yet offers a new dimension and opportunity for extended study. It is not a "stand alone" activity. Every child should be familiar with its power and potential.

When students in our fourth-grade class access the Internet, research on-line resources, or communicate with other schools, they are using the technology and the Internet as a learning vehicle for meeting one of our instructional objectives—using the Internet to engage children in discovery as a function of the specific curriculum. The Internet is the product of the process created by the computer and modem, and other computers and modems around the world. One of the interesting aspects of this innovation is that what the Internet is today will, most likely, be quite different tomorrow as it evolves, changes, and grows. The power of the Internet continues, yet our ability to use it exists only when our computer and modem are turned on.

As a Parent

As a parent, you want the "best" for your children—this includes exposing them to this *now* technology of information resources. Perhaps you want to learn alongside your children. This is important, because when you understand the potential and power of this exciting social and educational change, a commonality will exist in teaching and learning. As well, if you feel the education system in your area, public or private, isn't providing your children with the necessary knowledge skills related to computers and technology, you will have the "know-how" to take matters into your own hands.

And, admit it, there are probably other reasons. The Internet is quickly becoming the shopping mall of the future. Already, thousands of entrepreneurs are hocking everything from computers to kids' toys. It is becoming the place for quick, hassle-free perusing and purchasing for those in the know. With credit card security problems being remedied, the Internet may be the biggest boon to business since commercial media advertising. For those in business, it is a profit opprtunity; for the consumer, it means choice and competition.

And it's becoming very chic to have an Internet address. Friends are impressed when you can recite your e-mail address after a 16-kilometer jog. Looks great on your business card, too. Just saying, "dot com" makes you feel special! Seriously, information in our society translates to opportunity, influence, and even power. Access is equity, and barriers to this access may create disparities in knowledge and understanding. It is important, therefore, that all who want access to the information are able to obtain it.

As a Kid

For kids, the Internet is both a preparation for later and a conduit to the adventure of learning that allows immediate and worthwhile educational experiences.

WHAT DO WE REALLY NEED TO DO THIS?

We assume you have had a bit of experience using a computer. Whether you have also had some experience as a telecommunicator or this is your first time, become familiar with this section. One of our goals is to make you feel confident as you embark on your journey. Use the resources that are available. Ask lots of questions. Question are good. See page 24 for contacts, or e-mail us. We may not know all the answers, but it will be nice chatting with you. With this in mind, we will briefly review the essentials that make the Internet work. You might know much of this already. But if not, it's quite simple.

Computer

Yes, you need a computer, but it doesn't necessarily have to be yours. It can be owned by a school, friend, business, or significant other. That's the good part. It can be a Macintosh, or an IBM or IBM-compatible, which are generically referred to as PCs. (Macintosh has introduced the Power PC, compatible with IBM. It gets a little confusing, but don't worry about it now.) You need not have a new computer to enter the Information Superhighway. We started on a MacSE. However, do check with a computer store or the company that will be your provider, and tell them what you have and find out if it is compatible with your software (especially the amount of RAM it takes to run the thing). You'll need a minimum of 4 megabytes of RAM (8 is preferable, but check with your local computer educator/mentor teacher or computer retailer). Many new computers are sold with 500 megabytes of storage space on the hard drive. As programs and tasks become more complex, the need for greater computer memory increases. You really don't need to know how everything works, at least at the beginning. It is nice to know, and your credibility will jump immensely, but you can still successfully use the Internet if you simply know how to recognize the keyboard and can point and click. So, don't worry about bits, bytes, megabytes, or gigabits right now. There's time for that when you're cruising along this amazing highway.

Dedicated Phone Line

A dedicated phone line is a *single* telephone line (not one of those clusters that schools usually have in the office) that enters your classroom, or home, and is necessary if you want to telecommunicate without being disconnected whenever someone picks up the phone. Even with Call Waiting, you will need to use the No Call Waiting command, but that is a minor inconvenience. You'll find one phone at home just isn't enough anymore (especially with preteens or teens), so get ready for one more basic service charge. But it is great not having to compete with anyone for the phone line! One of the realities with school is that teachers don't have their own telephones. Almost every other desk in the world has a phone on it, but not that of the teacher. One of the early obstacles that we will encounter, and change, is this way of thinking. Those with influence need to understand that the phone (not the instrument, only the line) has become a learning tool of the twentieth century. If this is perceived as a problem at your school, present your proposal for telecommunications to the principal, PFA (Parent Faculty Association) or PTA (Parent-Teachers' Association), local boosters group, or neighboring business. Ask for "seed" money for this worthwhile endeavor. In most cases, they who ask shall receive! For home use, ask the kids to kick in for part of it. When they're done laughing hysterically, open your own purse or wallet and order the second line.

Phone Modem

Modem is an interesting word that finds its origin in **Mo**dulate/ **Dem**odulate, which translates to "varying the amplified frequency, or phase of a carrier, wave, or signal." (We think that means the varying tonal pitch in that "screeching" sound you hear when you are sending or receiving something using your modem.) The modem is the little box (it's rectangular in shape and comes in several appealing designer colors—computer-gray, computer-beige, computer-chrome, computer-black, and other exciting decor-matching hues) that either sits by your computer or is internally installed (in which case it is not a box, but a card). The modem translates the computer language into a phone language or sound that can be sent across the phone line, and then translates it back into a computer language at the destination. If you ever hear the sound made by a modem, you'll understand why dogs and horses scamper to the hills in fright. However, it is the modem that liberates you and your computer to the "outside world." So, if not connected already, connect the external modem to the computer and to the phone jack (using the cords that will only go in the correct holes and plugs) and you're nearly ready to begin. A small "Y" jack (about one dollar from a hardware store) in the phone socket will allow you to plug your phone and the modem in the same line, so you won't need to keep plugging in and unplugging your phone and computer every time you want to use either the phone or computer. But remember, you cannot use the phone to talk and the modem to telecommunicate at the same time (the instructions for the modem are very clear and it's a very simple procedure to do).

Fiber Optics, Ethernet & Transceivers

These are other ways of sending and receiving information. Installation of fiber optics and Ethernet at home and/or school speeds up the information at an impressive rate. (Ethernet is a common networking scheme used to link computers together so that data can be shared.) If you happen to be at a school where they have this service, you and your students will be able to work at a much greater speed, thus allowing more students access within a given period of time. That can mean a great deal to a teacher who is planning schedules for thirty or so kids. (If you should be in this enviable position, the connecting technician will install an Ethernet card and a transceiver if they were not installed in your computer at the factory. They're nice to have, but not essential for accessing the Internet.)

Furniture

Once you get your computer, you need to set it on something. In your classroom, find an out-of-the-way spot near the wall where the electrical outlets are present. If your school was built during the last twenty years, you may have outlets in the floor. Secure a sturdy table (computer tables aren't necessary) where your computer, printer, and other peripheral and materials can be held. Find a chair that seems to be the right height for the kids and probably one for you, too.

At home, imagine a dark wood-grained paneled den filled with books, brass artifacts, and an air of social position. Back to reality—for most of us, a folding table, work desk, or a strong table from an office discount store will do. It really doesn't matter, as long as it holds the computer and the assortment of peripherals that you will accumulate. Test the table legs for sturdiness (you need not have your kids do a kneeling pyramid on the table top). Just press on it and shake it a little. If it's your previous work desk, just clear away some of the mess (a cardboard box is good for "cleaning up").

Software

You're probably wondering, "What software do I need so I can get on the Internet?" Good question. You'll need software to access the provider (to dial-in and connect) and software to use as an interface to travel around the Internet. It's quite simple with the new "user-friendly" packages. We did it, and that says something. Most likely, you'll get your software when you sign up for the service or provider—and we have suggestions on how you can get a fine bargain on that part as well.

You'll probably be given Netscape or Mosaic, or something similar, to provide a graphic interface with the Internet. This is so you will be able

to see all the pictures, and move about this network with the greatest
of ease. Commercial on-line services like Prodigy, America Online,
and CompuServe come with easy-to-install software.

If you can't afford your own equipment, there are other ways to get on
the Internet. Call the local library and see if they have Internet access.
More and more public libraries are installing computers with Internet
access for the client. Or you might try a local coffee house. (In fact,
that's where we meet to talk about the Internet.) Scores of coffee
houses from Nantucket to Winnipeg are serving up the Internet with a
rich cup of Java. Nice concept.

ACCESSING THE INTERNET

Entry to the Internet is far less complicated than it was even a year or
two ago. Now the on-ramps are positioned almost everywhere. There
are easy entry points and there are very easy entry points. One of the
simplest methods for accessing the Internet is through a commercial
multi-use service like Prodigy, America Online, CompuServe, eWorld,
or Microsoft telecommunications services. All are *extremely* user
friendly and easy to install. They also have many other uses, so you
will be exposed to many telecommunication resources with one
subscription and a fairly reasonable fee. Commercial services are
racing to provide easy access and full-service Internet hookups. They
are feeling the pressure from a near-frantic populace as well as a
frenetic industry that is becoming very competitive (that's good for
you). In many cases, when using these "all-purpose" services, you
will find that time and access are limited and connections are slower.
But a commercial service is certainly a viable entry point, and one in
which you are guaranteed to have success. That in itself is worth a
great deal.

Soaring up like weeds after a spring shower (did we really say that?) are independent Internet providers for those who just want to get on the Internet with full access, top speed, and an easy-to-use yet sophisticated interface. Don't be afraid—they are easy and intended to reach "the rest of us" for this amazing journey. Look through the Yellow Pages under Computer Networks, Internet, Computer Bulletin Boards, and/or Telecommunications. Call a few of these eager entrepreneurs and ask pertinent questions as to cost, educational discount (don't be shy, do it, and do it the first time), length of service, guarantees, trial period, full access, local connect charges, trouble shooting, and customer service. Draw a grid and begin your comparison with four or five of those located in your community. Be sure to ask what their background is. Of course it isn't necessary, but it's always of value if one of the employees has some prior experience with education, and especially curriculum. Another access point may be education offices. More county and district offices are entering the information age and are attempting to form consortiums and networks within the county/district school system. A few phone calls may yield tremendous rewards. As well, a local university may wish to adopt your school or classroom and allow you remote access to their computer system. Almost every major university in the world is now part of the Internet. A wonderful resource is just to be able to communicate from one university to another across the globe. As an Internet user, you have equal access to these rich resources (see American Universities and Colleges and Universities Around the World on page 142).

The state or provincial departments of education (and State University System in the United States) may have networks that you can connect to for a nominal fee. We found a public server in California where educators can access the Internet for only $50.00 per year. Be sure to check for speed and overload issues—if the system slows down at certain periods during the day because of the number of people using it, make sure you are aware of this before you commit for the long term. To be effective, you need to be able to "connect" to the service at all times.

CONNECTING

Once you are connected with all systems properly functioning, it's a matter of clicking on the software and bringing the Internet interface to your screen. The process is generally the same. You type in your I.D. and password (provided to you when you subscribe to a service) and you then bring up the home page of your provider or interface. The interfaces most people are using are Netscape or Mosaic, but there are others. Follow the instructions for your software and you will soon be searching, clicking, exploring, and learning. If you are randomly looking here and there, you will find sites that may be of great interest or some of little value, but keep going.

What It Will Cost

The cost of these services differs significantly, so be sure to use your grid and mark in the specific costs and services provided by each. And remember, ask for a "teachers' discount," even if you will be using the service at home for "planning." (In our survey we were able to get a 50% discount off the $20.00 connection fee and $30.00 monthly fee.) It isn't a bad deal to get the software and be connected for $25.00, get 150 hours on the Internet, then pay a $15.00 monthly service fee.

WHO PAYS?

Teachers

Ask the principal. If your principal has an inkling about future educational quality programming, he or she should be able to quickly take your case to the district and secure the required monthly service fee. If the budget is decentralized, then it should be no problem at all, as it is a school site decision. Remember to tap the PFA and PTA or a local business/corporation. This minimal outlay should not be the barrier for implementation. (We'll even phone your principal, if you ask nicely.)

Parents

As a parent, reach a little deeper, but do understand what you are really providing to your children. This is not to make you feel that if you don't go on the Internet your child will be condemned to remedial classes all through school. But if you do expose your children to the Internet, they will come to an understanding of a new way to think about learning and data collection. They may even embrace it as a wonderful and motivating activity and feel that school has value after all. Few lessons in school or life have the potential of such a dramatic outcome. In other words, skip take-out food once per month and the Internet is a household word.

Kids

If you want your parents to pay for this, simply tell them that what you learn on the Internet will prepare you for the future and ensure you are awarded a scholarship to the best university. That should do the trick. Or, earn the money and pay for it yourself!

AS A TEACHER

Can I Access the Internet at Home as Well as in My Classroom?

As long as you have a computer, modem, and software installed at home, you can access your school account from there. Much of your preparation in all subjects occurs at home or away from your classroom. You will be previewing many sites out of class that will later be incorporated into your lessons. You do not need to purchase separate software since you are using this for the same purpose. Just install it at both places. Whenever telecommunications is occurring, you are using an I.D. and personal password for access. If you have the same software installed at home as at school, you simply replicate the process at home as you do at school. Just be certain you haven't violated any licensing agreements for multiple software use, or school district policies.

You can also get much fancier and purchase specific software that will let you tap into your office Ethernet (if you should have this in your room). If this is the case, consult with your district technology mentor for assistance.

AS A PARENT

How Can We Access the Internet From Home?

Look closely at your computer. Rub your hands over the cool fan vents and note the serene, calm climate that surrounds your space. You might even sit down in front of the screen and just look around. Remember this moment. Soon the Internet will come alive, and you and the kids will be vying for time and space. You are not immune!

Okay, okay, you'll give the kids equal time, but once you pull the
blankets over those young shoulders, you'll be cruising from Victoria
to Auckland. Before you know it, midnight will have come and gone.

When you set up a personal account from home, you need to find a
suitable provider for your particular needs. Try to get a discount for
being a classroom helper, student, Girl Scout /Girl Guide leader, soccer
coach, member of the Auto Club, or a card-carrying member of the Sea
World Shamu Fan Club. It doesn't really matter, as long as you ask (if
you don't want a discount and like paying retail, please do so, or mail
the difference to charity). Many providers do not as yet have discount
policies, so they are making them up as they go along. Just act like this
is the thing that is expected. They won't know the difference.

Think about a reasonable number of hours per month that you actually
may be "browsing" around the Internet. You may not know this now,
which is why a trial period is probably good. A commercial business
may be on-line from eight to ten hours a day, but for home use three
hours a day would probably suffice. Also, providers should have
different fee schedules for household accounts and business accounts.

Remember, prices vary, so shop and compare. Even if you can afford
the higher price, it is good modeling for your kids to see you research
before you "buy."

AS A KID

How Can I Access the Internet Without My Parents or Teachers Standing Over My Shoulder?

There are some things you can do to have greater independence on the
Internet. Let your parents know what your goals are and what it is you
are trying to do. Be honest. Ask them if they have any concerns and

discuss those concerns without rolling your eyes. Next, respect their concerns and assure them that you have no intention of violating these issues. Describe what you need from them, which might be, for example, privacy on e-mail. Ask them if they can respect your needs on this point (although a great temptation, parents are not permitted to roll their eyes). As all of you in the family will be on the Internet in the home setting, begin to share worthwhile "traveling" experiences with each other. This is like telling travel stories. Again, respect the choices of each, even if Mom and Dad want to show you the National Art Gallery in London, and you want to share concert reviews of your favorite rock group. We're sure there are many discoveries that you won't want to share and that's okay, too, as long as they are within the guidelines of what you both agreed would be acceptable browsing. Remember, it is politically beneficial to let your parents know how much this experience is contributing to your educational and social development and that you will probably get into a great college because of this exposure. Enough said. Enjoy, share, have fun, and, on occasion, say, "Thank you."

WHAT YOU'LL FIND ON THE INTERNET

Weave your way onto the Internet and you will find more than you imagined. You can order a pizza, with or without anchovies, and have it delivered to your door in forty-five minutes; peruse cookbooks and castles, mushrooms or museums; visit your favorite planet; or play Monopoly where you can buy Park Place. It's all here and growing every minute. If you can think of a topic to study, or a place to visit, you will probably find it on the Internet. What is most impressive about the Internet and telecommunications technology is what it does to the user. You'll find yourself both a teacher and a learner on a journey of discovery, inquiry, and knowledge. Once you embark, you can never turn back.

A TEAM SPORT

Contrary to popular belief, using a computer, telecommunications, and, specifically, the Internet need not be a "solo" experience. Being on-line encourages cooperative exploration, sharing, and collaboration. Teachers would surely consider two-person research and data collection teams as positive experiences. Together, you will browse, explore previously "discovered" sites, and find new and uncharted territory. More than likely, you'll find the Internet a powerful vehicle for creating or maintaining motivation for educational growth and development. Note what happens, then let us know.

SOME CAUTION

For Teachers & Parents

A diverse population uses the Internet—international organizations, national museums, universities, research institutes, public agencies, businesses, students, revolutionaries, as well as children. You will want to use much of the available content in your classroom or at home; you will not want your students or child to view some of the content. This is similar to issues related to appropriate programming of commercial and cable television, movies, and videos. Make clear what is acceptable and what is not. Material of a sexual, violent, or profane nature has no place in the classroom or on the home computer of a young child. Initially, you may want to instruct children as to what sites they can visit. To complete our goals of self-initiating problem solving and the identification of appropriate resources, however, students must be permitted to move freely around the Internet to make choices and decisions related to their own learning.

As teachers and parents, it is up to you to guide the "site-seer" to suitable use. That is another reason why you should be fully informed

about this technology. You will set the tone related to the materials
and sites that can be viewed and downloaded. Make this clear
from day one, and your children will comply with your reasonable
expectations.

SUBJECT ARTICULATION

Randomness is wonderful, but teachers, parents, and kids want
and need resources that complement and supplement curriculum
requirements and related topics of interest. In *Site Seeing the
Internet*, we have placed the Internet sites in categories by subject
area. In some cases they may overlap (as might be expected in a
thematic interdisciplinary approach).

TO SEARCH OR NOT TO SEARCH

There Really Is No Question

Visiting sites on the Internet is like using an around-the-world airline
ticket—you can go wherever you want, whenever you want. As you
travel, you will stop at sites called URLs (Uniform Resource Locators).
These are links to network services within documents. The first part
of the URL before the two slashes (//) specifies the method of access.
The second is usually the address of the computer where the information or service is located. For example, the URL for the Smithsonian
Institution in Washington, D.C. is *http://www.si.edu/*. Each of the
designations between a dot or slash represents a direction or location
on the Internet. In combination, these direct your computer to a
specific subject site. This will not be immediately important to you,
but we did want you to have a resource if you should question what all
those lines, slashes, and dots mean. How many sites are there? There
are certainly hundreds of thousands, soon to be millions. Some of

these sites are stable, or what are called "Blue Chip" sites that will be with us for a long time. Others have a shorter life, and will be removed by their creators or pushed aside for lack of interest. In this book, we have tried to find and note those sites that are both interesting and enduring.

HOW TO SEARCH

When you are looking for something on the Internet, you use keywords to search for information. Think about what it is you want to know more about, and what specific words describe it. For example, if you're interested in horses, you need to think of words that can help your search. In the space provided, you might type in words like *horse, horses, equine, thoroughbred*. List only one or two words at a time—too many words in a search will confuse the "search engine" (topic research indexes) and yield little data. (The most common search engines are InfoSeek, Yahoo, WebCrawler, and Lycos. Without such organizational indexes that can search in seconds, you would spend months, if not years, just trying to find topics randomly placed here and there.) In our example, the search of the word *horse* brings up a myriad of information sites about horses, breeds, colors, care, and so on. With a simple click, the description and the actual site soon appears on your screen. You have arrived.

In the following section, you'll find over two hundred sites that we feel provide a rich introduction to the Internet. And you don't have to search! We have provided you with the addresses, or URLs; all you have to do is type in the Internet address (example: http://www.yahoo.com/), click, and your journey will begin. Be sure to read your software instructions so you know how to save favorite addresses for future use (in Netscape, for example, you use Bookmark to save site addresses.)

SEARCHING THE INTERNET

Let's take a closer look. We assume you have loaded Netscape (see below), Mosaic, or other similar interface and are now on the Internet, on the home page. (If you are trying to do this with a text-only interface, you will get text, but miss on all the color, pictures, and pizzazz.) Find the space prefaced by the word Location (on Netscape it's near the top of the screen). Type in the URL address you want to visit, click your mouse (or hit the return key), and the search is on! In a few seconds, the home page of the site you're looking for will cover your screen, offering you choices related to the topic, or "links" to other sites that are connected in some way. This is where the fun begins and the dinner gets cold—or doesn't get cooked at all.

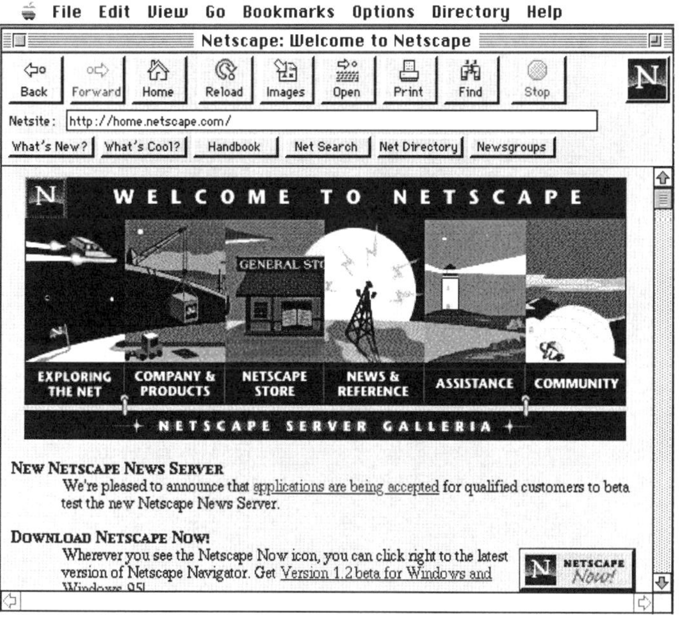

Occasionally, you may get a screen message that says "busy," "host not located," "not found," or something similar. Simply click on the button labeled "Back" or "Forward" (at the top of your screen) and try again. If you keep getting the message, wait a few minutes and give it another try. Although some site servers are officially "neutralized," many are down for a day or two or have moved. So don't give up right away.

SEARCH ENGINES

Find What You're Looking For

The Internet is a tremendous resource but sometimes finding what you want is like looking for a needle in a haystack. Don't worry. That's what search engines are for (see page 20). Some of the more common search engines are:

Yahoo
http://www.yahoo.com

WebCrawler
http://webcrawler.com

InfoSeek
http://www.infoseek.com

Lycos
http://www.lycos.com

PERSONAL SITE JOURNAL

You'll soon be perusing the Internet on your own. For sites you want to return to time and time again, you can save the address by using Bookmark (see page 20). Or you can use the grid below to jot down the site URL for later reference or to share with your best friend.

Site Description	URL/Address

JOURNALS, ORGANIZATIONS, RESOURCES & TECHNICAL SUPPORT

The following is a list of journals, organizations, and other resources you might find helpful on your tour of the Internet. Add to this list when you find other useful sources.

CUE /Journal
Computer Using Educator's Inc.
1210 Marina Village Parkway, Suite 100
Alameda, CA 94501

Electronic Learning
c/o Scholastic Inc.
555 Broadway
New York, NY 10012-3999

Net Guide
P.O. Box 420355
Palm Coast, FL 32142-9371

Internet World
P.O. Box 713
Mt. Morris, IL 61054
1-800-573-3062

PC Magazine
P.O. Box 54093
Boulder, CO 80321-4093
1-800-289-0429

MacWarehouse Catalog
(Great discounts on all computer equipment and peripherals)
P.O. Box 3013
17 Oak Street
Lakewood, NJ 08710
1-800-255-6227

Prodigy
445 Hamilton Avenue
White Plains, NY 10601
1-800-PRODIGY

Microsoft Service
One Microsoft Way
Redmond, WA 98052
1-206-882-8080

America Online
8619 Westwood Center Drive
Vienna, VA 22182
1-800-827-6364

eWorld
Apple Computer
P.O. Box 4493
Bridgeton, MO 63044-9718

CompuServe
P.O. Box 20212
Columbus, OH 43220
1-800-848-8199

Netscape Communication Corporation
501 East Middlefield Road
Mountain View, CA 94043
info@netscape.com

ISTE (International Society for Technology in Education)
iste@oregon.uoregon.edu
http://isteonline.uoregon.edu

The authors' e-mail addresses:
gmgarfield@csupomona.edu
smcdono@cyberg8t.com

The Tour
Begins Here....

WEB
SITES

WEB
SITES

WEB
SITES

WEB
SITES

MOSTLY MUSEUMS

THE WEB MUSEUM
100,000 Visitors a Week

http://sunsite.unc.edu/louvre

Over 100,000 visitors a week tour this amazing site. Over 5 million documents are delivered to those who enter. You'll be astonished with special exhibits such as Gothic Art, Cézanne, and Medieval Art that are on display in the temporary exhibit hall. Explore the general exhibits throughout the Web Museum, as well as the many other rich resources. Remember, this is the Louvre and you are in Paris, so while you're here, click on the tour of this wonderful romantic city. You'll be glad you did.

LEONARDO DA VINCI
Amazing!

http://www.leonardo.net/main.html

Here, at the Leonardo da Vinci Museum, you can view some of the most famous art works of all time. This award-winning site displays paintings, drawings, inventions, and other works by the great painter, designer, scientist, futurist, and thinker, Leonardo da Vinci. It's well worth the visit!

VATICAN EXHIBIT
How the City Came Back to Life

**http://sunsite.unc.edu/expo/
vatican.exhibit/exhibit/Main_Hall.html**

Settle in, have a cappuccino and biscotti, and join us on a visit
to the Vatican Web Site. (You'll actually be at the famous Vatican
Exhibit in the Library of Congress in Washington, D.C.) From the
Main Hall, read about the archeology, medicine, biology, and
music of ancient Rome. Visit the Vatican library or view a five-
hundred-year-old manuscript. Take a journey back through time
to one of the most amazing historical places in the world.

SMITHSONIAN'S NATIONAL AIR &
SPACE MUSEUM
"Hey, Orvil"

http://www.nasm.edu/PA/Exhibits.html

Catch a glimpse of the Wright Brothers' 1903 Flyer, the "Spirit of
St. Louis" (Jimmy Stewart is nowhere to be found), the Apollo
11 command module, and John Glenn's Mercury spacecraft. See
pictures, get information, and be part of the history. Learn about
the air and space explorers who defied the cynics who said,
"Man will never fly." Not only did man fly, but so did women!
Join us as we lift to the skies. The tour departs immediately on
runway WWW! Last boarding call.

AMERICAN PRESIDENTS
To the Library, If You Please

http://sunsite.unc.edu/lia/president/

This site is the official passport to the modern presidential libraries. Visit the libraries with related exhibits of U.S. presidents from Herbert Hoover to George Bush. View a variety of archives and collections. This fascinating site includes some American First Ladies as well.

ART FROM THE FOURTH
MILLENNIUM B.C.
Krannert Art Museum

http://www.art.uiuc.edu/kam/

Until recently, viewing art from thousands of years ago was a privilege that belonged to the few who could afford the time and resources to visit the world's greatest art depositories. Now, you can access these treasures from your computer! At this site, you can tour the permanent collection that includes American, European, Asian and African, Pre-Columbian and Near Eastern, and twentieth-century art. Special presentations, exhibitions, and other events are listed, as well as great surprises. Give yourself time to browse around. Visualize the life and times that may have occurred while the work was being created. Have fun, learn, and take a break at the museum snack shop.

LIFE OVER TIME
Teeth, Tusks & Tarpits!

**http://rs6000.bvis.uic.edu:80/museum/
Home.html**

At this site, located at The Field Museum of Natural History in Illinois, you can be part of an interactive exhibit, take the delightful tour Life Before Dinosaurs, learn about fossils, and (for teachers) sample some of the lesson plans. This site is always a winner with kids, parents, and teachers. Slip back in time and join in the discoveries.

GLENBOW MUSEUM
A Canadian Jewel

**http://www.lexicom.ab.ca/~glenbow/
museum.htm**

The Glenbow houses historical, ethnological, and military collections, as well as mineralogy and art collections. The art collection is superb and you can view contemporary Canadian art and a unique Native Art exhibit. The Glenbow, western Canada's largest museum, includes archives and a library.

GUIDE TO MUSEUMS & CULTURAL RESOURCES
Around the World on Every Continent

http://www.usc.edu/lacmnh/webmuseums/

Africa, the Middle East, Europe, Asia, Australia, North America,
Antarctica, South America—wherever you may be, this is the
site of museums around the world. Some links provide just
information, some have extensive databases, while others enable
you to view images of actual works within the museums. The site
is a great source for the browsers in your classroom or family.

THE SMITHSONIAN
Visit Washington, D.C.

http://www.si.edu/

The Smithsonian is a group of museums and libraries majesti-
cally placed in and around the National Mall in Washington,
D.C. Now, without leaving your computer, you and your kids can
travel to one of Washington's main tourist attractions and glean
the gems of history from one of the world's most famous archives. Your cybervisit may include museums, galleries, and
research centers in and about the U.S. capital. As well, you'll
find resources to assist you in your study of the diverse cultures
living in the United States. We guarantee you'll be back often. As
every visitor says, "One visit to the Smithsonian isn't enough to
scratch the surface."

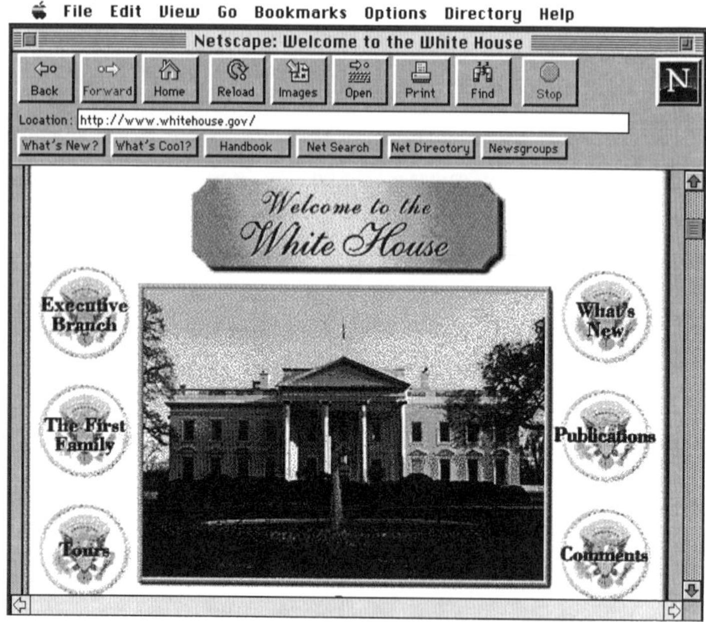

WELCOME TO THE WHITE HOUSE
Please Enter Through the Cyber Door

http://www.whitehouse.gov/

No need to scale the fence to visit this house. Simply type in the address and you will be delivered to the front door, past the secret service. Tours await (with no admission ticket, longlines, or summer humidity) that whisk you from room to room, let you hear from the American president and vice president, allow you to peruse publications, and let you in on some new secrets related to the First Family and, of course, life in the big white house on Pennsylvania Avenue. Knock, knock! Anyone home?

MAMMOTHS AND SABER-TOOTHED CATS
The George C. Page Museum & La Brea Tar Pits

http://www.usc.edu/lacmnh/page

This interesting museum site shows what life in Los Angeles, California was like 10,000-40,000 years ago, during the Ice Age (burrr!). Saber-toothed cats and mammoths roamed the basin where L.A. is located today. Outside the museum are the world-famous La Brea tar pits where unsuspecting animals, while seeking water, were entombed. Today, archeological exploration continues within the city. This site also provides links to some exciting virtual exhibits on paleontology and archeology.

ART IN THE NEW WORLD
National Museum of American Art

http://www.nmaa.si.edu/

Here, you have access to a tremendous collection of North American art, spanning several centuries. Students can use this collection to enhance current studies of the Great Masters. Plans for this site include daily additions and growth, which could make it one of the great Internet museums. Begin your tour today, but be sure to check back often to see what has been added.

FANTASTIC BEASTS
Natural History Museum of Los Angeles County

http://www.usc.edu/lacmnh/departments/libraries/beasts/beasts.html

At this site, children will learn about the great mammals of the world and what these animals were like. The pictures were painted from descriptions provided by early explorers as they tried to explain what they had seen to artists. The images are interactive and require only a click to see and learn more, offering interesting lesson possibilities for kids.

CYBER SCIENCE

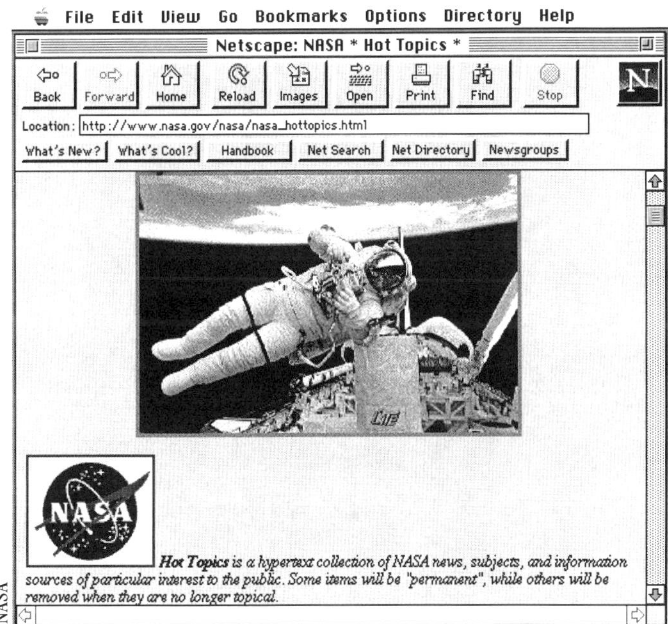

NASA
Hot Topics

http://www.nasa.gov/nasa/
nasa_hottopics.html

Stop in at the National Aeronautics and Space Administration for
a look-see at what's hot and what's not! Check Today at NASA for
the latest happenings and information. There are enough photos
(the quality of lunar and space photography is truly magical)
and information to make any space explorer "wannabee" crave
for more. Fascinating for the rest of us as well. Be sure to wear
your space suit.

VIEWS OF THE SOLAR SYSTEM
Planets I Have Known

**http://www.c3.lanl.gov/~cjhamil/
SolarSystem/**

This tour brings the heavenly bodies to your screen with a click of a planet. You'll be astonished at the visuals and the information available on the sun, moon, planets, asteroids, comets, and meteoroids. Make sure you search through the archive History of Space Exploration (including People Who Made a Contribution). This site, with great links to many other space stations, will satisfy the curiosity of all galactic adventurers. Get ready for blast off from your launch, uh, mouse pad. Zero minus five, four, three, two . . .

CURRENT WEATHER MAPS
"Raindrops Keep Falling On My Head"

http://rs560.cl.msu.edu/weather/

This site has up-to-date weather maps from every angle. Collect information from all over the world. View the weather via panel radar, infrared, and worldwide composite. Weather makes a fascinating study and naturally initiates problem solving and prediction. Does it snow in Morocco?

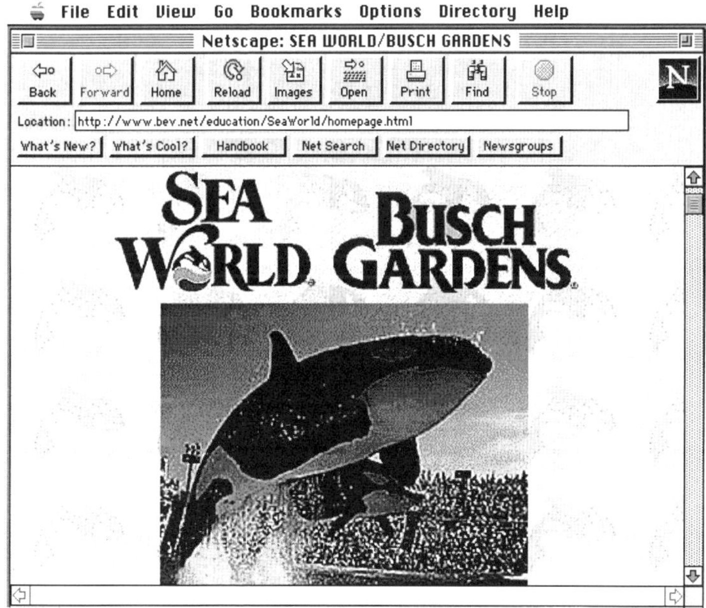

ANIMAL INFORMATION DATABASE
Sea World/Busch Gardens

http://www.bev.net/education/SeaWorld/homepage.html

Check out this site for the ever expanding Sea World/Busch
Garden education series. Study baleen and beluga whales, killer
whales, bottlenose dolphins; coral and coral reefs; walruses,
polar bears, and gorillas; and other endangered species. Teacher's guides are available. This source is committed to education,
the appreciation of science, and respect for all living creatures.
Sign on and begin to make a difference in the world.

HEART TO HEART
A Pump that Beats Two-and-a-Half Billion Times

http://sln.fi.edu/biosci/heart.html

No machine has the power or longevity of the human heart. Visit this site and learn more about this amazing body organ. While you're here, you'll also learn about the blood and what it does to sustain and maintain life, and other important information you should know about to maintain a healthy heart. (A great site to review just prior to your circulatory system test in science.)

ROCK & ROLL (THE EARTHQUAKE SITE)
The Seismological Laboratory (California Institute of Technology)

http://www.gps.caltech.edu/seismo/ seismo.page.html

Your first visit to this site could be in the early morning after a shaker, when everyone is standing around in sweatshirts trying to figure out how big the earthquake was and where the epicenter was. Here, you're guaranteed to enhance your knowledge of earthquakes. You'll learn, for example, that it's not unusual for southern California to experience 300 earthquakes a day (little ones, of course). Kids, especially, are fascinated by earthquakes, and knowledge of these events lessens anxiety and promotes greater understanding of the process. This site will turn you on your head with interesting facts, pictures, and information. Come shake, rattle, and roll with us at this site (grab the duct tape and the fish bowl.)

THE MAJESTIC WOLF
The Wolf Studies Project

http://informns.k12.mn.us/wolf.html

The Wolf Studies Project is an Internet-based activity that brings
life, nature, and the reality of learning clearly into the classroom. Here, you will follow the majestic wolf, gaining insight
into its habitat and lifestyle in the wild. Kids gravitate toward
this site, as it sets the foundation for further on-line and in-class
nature studies. Follow the tracks to this special site.

PET PAGES
Arf, Arf...Meow, Meow
(this is an equal opportunity
presentation)

**http://www.dynamo.net/dynamo/pets/
pets.html**

Every child has a story to tell about his or her pet, or a story
about someone else's pet (or, perhaps, a story about a trip to
the doctor because of an allergic reaction to a pet). Some of the
fun activities in this site are Put Your Pet On the Web, viewing
pet images, and talking about your pet. Remember, pets aren't
just dogs and cats. Perhaps you have an iguana or a lizard.
Share your pet with others on the Pet Pages.

ANIMAL PICTURES
Courtesy of the Smithsonian

**http://sunsite.unc.edu/pub/multimedia/
pictures/smithsonian/gif89a/science-
nature/**

This site brings pages and pages of animal images (gifs)
to your computer screen. There are many to choose from:
ants to buffalo, deer to snails. Admission is free, and as a bonus,
you don't need to clean up after them! You and your kids can
have an entire zoo at your fingertips. Post the pictures on the
walls and watch as interest, reading, and motivation increase.
Have fun.

MORE SPACE STUFF FROM THE NASA/
KENNEDY SPACE CENTER
Give Me Space!

http://www.ksc.nasa.gov/ksc.html

Everyone loves space, space adventures, and space stories, both
fiction and nonfiction. This site is full of exciting information
about space, specifically those questions related to space
servers, archives, the Space Center library, and ecological
issues. This site provides students with new avenues of problem
solving and decision making. With links to several other home
pages, this is truly an information center.

THE SIERRA CLUB
One Earth, One Chance

http://www.sierraclub.org

If you're concerned about social and ecological issues, this site is for you. The Sierra Club site provides a trail to critical issues facing environmentalist who are desperately trying to turn the tide of ecological destruction. Learn from members, find resources, and get involved. For over a hundred years the Sierra Club has been trying to make a difference. Find out more. Click the Sierra Club (student affiliations) and help save the planet.

THE NORTHERN LIGHTS
Did Someone Leave the Lights On?

http://www.geo.mtu.edu/weathr/aurora

Discover information links and images related to the beautiful, mysterious northern lights. The information at this site is abundant and the pictures are superb.

THE DAILY PLANET
(It's Not in Metropolis)

http://wx3.atmos.uiuc.edu/

Stop in at this site and explore weather, satellite maps, and the atmosphere. This is a university site for kids, and is being updated on a regular basis. Be sure to check back periodically.

ROCKHOUNDS
The Hardest Bark You'll Ever Hear

**http://www.rahul.net/infodyn/
rockhounds/rockhounds.html**

When you arrive at this site, climb in and around rocks, gems, and fossils. Visit the Museum of Minerology in Paris, jump to the Earth Department at the University of Calgary, or enter the National History Museum at Berne, Switzerland. You'll soon realize that this is a hard site to ignore.

WHALES: A THEMATIC WEB UNIT
A Whale of a Tale

**http://curry.edschool.Virginia.EDU:80/~kpj
5e/Whales/**

Everyone likes a good "tail," especially if it's connected to a great whale. This site combines one of children's favorite studies, the whale, with Internet resources. Included are teacher resources, student activities, whale projects, and other related topics. The actual lessons are here too! Thar she blows, mate!

WHALE NET
Bigger Than Your Mouse

http://whale.simmons.edu

Study whales without the salt air spray in your face. Here, you'll find information about the environment in which whales and other marine habitants of the world live. Researchers from all over share their research and data.

DIRECTORATE OF TIME
It's Time!

http://tycho.usno.navy.mil/clocks.html

What is real time? How do you know what time it really is?
Who do you ask for the accurate time? For astronauts who
rendezvous in space, timing is critical. You can't be late for a
date. Time is measured by an ensemble of 60 independently
operating Cesium atomic clocks and 7-10 hydrogen Maser
clocks. Precision is necessary for modern technology including
communications and navigation. Tick, tick, tick . . .

JASON PROJECT
Oh, Jason, Where Are You?

http://seawifs.gsfc.nasa.gov/
(Click to Jason Page)

The Jason projects are major scientific explorations for kids,
teachers, and parents using the now-famous remote camera
robot Jason to explore where few men, women, or children
have gone before. Follow the various projects to the Galapagos
Islands to explore unique marine life, the Mediterranean Sea
to examine an ancient Roman shipwreck, rainforests, the
changing sea, or a rare visit to the R.M.S. Titanic. Includes
discussion groups and teacher's guides. Remember that kid
in the class named Jason?

VOLCANOWORLD
Is There Really Such a Thing as a Volcanologist?

http://volcano.und.nodak.edu/

Volcanoes have amazed and fascinated scientists and students alike since the first volcano blew its top. Mountains form, islands appear, and the landscape changes forever as the molten fire spews forth. Visit this site and discover the volcanoes of the world, volcanic parks, and monuments. While you're here, read the Volcano News. Talk to a volcanologist and venture on a volcano search. This is one of the "hottest" sites on the Web.

THE VIRTUAL GARDEN
Plant Early But Watch for the Gophers

http://www.pathfinder.com/@@3avTcQAAA AAAACv6/vg/

Planting a garden as a class project or home hobby is always a worthwhile activity. This site contains magazines, books (Time Life Garden Library), public gardens, and plant societies. All the advice is here, whether your thumb is green or blue. Get in touch with your "roots."

GARDENING PROJECTS
If It's Been Done, It's Been Done by 4-H

gopher://gopher.ext.vt.edu:70/11/vce-data/hort/consumer/general/children/ 4hpubs

The address for this site is so long, your plants will grow to maturity while you type it in! This is a great site for exploring and learning from the dedicated youth of the 4-H clubs. It's all here: family gardening, pruning container gardens (perfect for classroom), garden ecology, herb gardens, nutrition, seeds and soils, urban gardens, vegetable gardens, and windowsill salad gardens. We aren't kidding when we call this a gopher site! Chomp!

THE STARCHILD PROJECT
Connecting NASA and the Classroom

**http://guinan.gsfc.nasa.gov/K12/
StarChild.html**

There is never enough space! Here is another space site, but this one is aimed specifically at children. On this journey, you'll explore the galaxies, the sun and moon, the planets, space, and for those adventuresome enough to go beyond, the universe. Great themes, wonderful photos, and real excitement for every space explorer.

GEMS & OTHER TREASURES
Gems & Minerals on Display

**http://galaxy.einet.net/images/gems/
gems-icons.html**

A truly magnificent collection of the world's most interesting gems and minerals. See the jewelry, sculptures, and diamonds. With lots of descriptions and visuals, this collection will amaze you with its beauty. Kids have always been fascinated with rocks, gems, and minerals. You will be, too.

RAINFOREST
You Can Change the World

http://www.ran.org/ran/

Half the earth's known plants and animals live deep within
the rainforest. This site introduces you to the mysteries and
marvels of the world's rainforests and shows what you can
do to save them. Learn about the vegetation, the animals, and
the people who live there. The site also includes a glossary, a
question-and-answer section, and resources for teachers and
kids. Join us under the canopy and save the forest.

THE WORLD THROUGH THE EYES OF A HONEY BEE
B-Eye

**http://cvs.anu.edu.au/andy/beye/
beyehome.html**

This site shows you what one researcher thinks a bee actually
sees. Although their view isn't what we would call multimedia,
it is interesting to see the world through different eyes. Hit the
B-Eye on this unusual site. (Who thinks of these things anyway?)

MONTEREY BAY AQUARIUM
Our Gold Fish Is Six Years Old

**http://www.usw.nps.navy.mil/~millercw/
aq/index.html**

You can dive to the depths of new knowledge as you enter the
Monterey Bay Aquarium, which showcases the world's most
diverse and spectacular marine life. You'll visit deep reefs,
rocky shores, and tide pools; have access to nearly a hundred
innovative habitat galleries and exhibits; and much, much more.
You won't want to miss the incredible Sea Otter Exhibit and the
Sea Otter Rescue and Conservation Program. Take a plunge and
learn about the fascinating underwater world of Monterey Bay.

TALK TO THE ANIMALS
The Electronic Zoo

http://netvet.wustl.edu/e-zoo.htm

This is the all-time, all-amazing animal resource page with facts, pictures, and information about all the animals. Learn everything you want to know about animals from ardvarks to zebras. For horse lovers, cow connoisseurs, and others, you'll find out what's new and what's gnu.

Ken Boschert

NIGHT OF THE IGUANA
My Friend Liz...ard

http://iguana.images.com/

An honest-to-goodness "Iguana Cam" takes pictures of an
iguana and makes them available to whoever drops in for a visit.
A new picture reloads every few minutes. Who would believe it?
Even an iguana can be a star! What a great world.

THE ON-LINE INSECT DATABASE
Don't Bug Me!

http://bluehen.ags.udel.edu/insects/
descriptions/entohome.html

Kids love bugs and crawly things. You will, too, after visiting this
site. There is more information than you ever wanted to know
about bugs. Great pictures and movies, too!

THE TELE-GARDEN
How Does Your Garden Grow?

http://cwis.usc.edu/dept/garden

No rabbit or ground squirrel will destroy this tele-robotic
garden. This is an amazing site that lets you plant, grow, and
tend to a garden on-line. Anyone can view this virtual garden.
Just keep the water off the computer.

GLOBAL GARDENS
Botanical Sites to Stroll Through & Enjoy

http://meena.cc.uregina.ca/~liushus/bio/botany.html

If you're looking for a plant, you'll find it in this growing site. For the budding botanist, this is true paradise. Information, location instructions, and pictures are sprouting up here. This is a comprehensive site that is updated regularly.

CLOUDS
I Think There Is a Song About Clouds

http://climate.gsfc.nasa.gov/~cahalan/FractalClouds/FractalClouds.html

Here, you'll find information and lots of visuals (photographs) on a fantastic variety of cloud forms and their implications for climate. This is a developing page with potential for teaching visitors a better understanding of what the various cloud types—cirrus, altocumulus, stratus, and cumulonimbus clouds—mean.

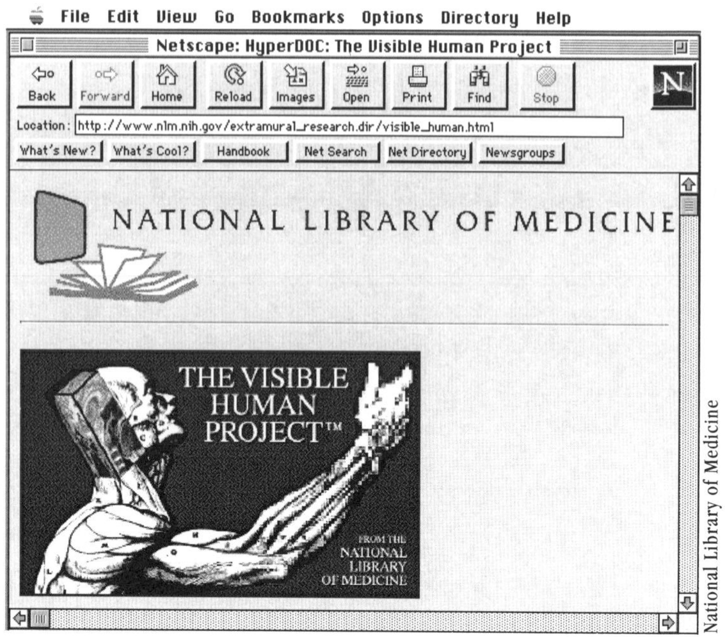

THE VISIBLE HUMAN PROJECT
Gone to Pieces

http://www.nlm.nih.gov/ extramural_research.dir/visible_human.html

Here, you'll find interesting, detailed, three-dimensional representations of the male and female human bodies. This site is sometimes referred to as the "cadaver project." You be the judge. Great for those interested in "real" anatomy and for future doctors. Check it out before entering the operating room.

ARE FRECKLES GENETIC?
Diving Into the Gene Pool

**http://www.exploratorium.edu/genepool/
genepool_home.html**

This site examines and explains DNA, then explores human's
relationships to other organisms, the ethics of genetic research,
inheritance, and more. When you visit this site, you'll learn why
kids have blue eyes or wear blue "genes."

ENVIRONMENT INFORMATION SERVERS
I Don't Like Air I Can See

**http://kaos.erin.gov.au/other_servers/
category/server_category.html**

This is a general or multiple-site page about the environment.
You'll find excellent links to many other servers on topics such
as geology, fauna, health, landscape, and global climate.

WELCOME TO ANTARCTICA
Ice and Climate

http://www.nbs.ac.uk/public/icd/

At this site, you'll find lots of information on ice and related
climates. The links are interesting and will extend your journey.
Be sure to see the satellite pictures of the Giant Iceberg.

A PHOTO GALLERY OF THE UNIVERSE
They Call Me Hubble. And You?

**http://www.stsci.edu/pubinfo/
BestOfHST95.html**

The Hubble Space Telescope (HST) sends back never-before-seen pictures of the universe. At this site, you'll see some of the best—they are truly spectacular. Check out Supernova 1987A, Orion Nebula, the Cartwheel Galaxy, Comet P/Shoemaker-Levy, Saturn Storm, and many more. "Scope" out this site for a truly stellar experience.

LASERS & LIGHTS
Laserium-Music for Your Eyes

http://www.laserium.com/

Stop here for a show of bright and unusual laser images. Laser technology is an expanding science and art form, and this site chronicles the changes that are occurring in this field. If you look closely on the far wall, you might see the imprint, "Luke Skywalker was here!"

HORSE COUNTRY
Bring a Bag of Carrots & a Firm Apple

**http://www.pathology.washington.edu/
Horse/Carroll_horse.html**

At this site, aimed at junior riders, you'll learn about horses through a combination of text, photography, and art. There are also links to other horse sites.

THE ELECTRONIC BIRD SITE
Bye, Bye Birdie

http://netvet.wustl.edu/birds.htm

Another reference from the Electronic Zoo (see page 55), but this time you'll visit the world of birds. This site has tons of information and pictures of birds. Look skyward and take flight to this intriguing place on the Internest (yes, we really said that!).

PENGUIN PAGE
Why Not? We All Love Penguins

**http://www.sas.upenn.edu/~kwelch/
penguin.html**

The whimsical penguin is a favorite. Read Penguin Facts and Tuxedo Humor to learn about these animals and how they have adapted to various environments. Study the wonderful photographs. You'll leave this site with a smile. And, your comments and impressions are welcome. That's nice.

BATS BATS BATS
Bat Conservation International

http://www.batcon.org/

At this site, click the bat button and learn everything there is to know about bats and packs of facts. The bat is an intriguing, misunderstood, and often maligned creature that must be protected. So, join us as we enter the strange world of the bat. You don't want to be left in the dark on this one.

THE GREAT WHITE SHARK
Everyone, Out of the Water!

http://ucmp1.berkeley.edu/Doug/shark.html

Nice images of the great white shark (if you're into this sort of thing, and kids usually are) with tremendous information related to the 400 million years that sharks have existed. Keep your hands and feet inside the boat!

THE ELECTRONIC PREHISTORIC SHARK MUSEUM
Body With No Bones

http://turnpike.net/emporium/C/celestial/epsm.htm

Here, you'll learn about sharks, and about paleontologists who reconstruct the life and history of the shark from the only remains available, fossilized teeth. Take a tour of this special museum.

THE SCIENCE LEARNING NETWORK
You Can Be the Next Ms. or Mr. Wizard

http://sln.fi.edu/tfi/sln/sln.html

The Science Learning Network is a collaborative effort of
schools, businesses, and museums intended to enhance the
learning and teaching of science, math, and technology in
the elementary and junior high classrooms. Virtual exhibits
are provided based on the center's specific areas of expertise.
See if you can discover what these might be!

Oregon Museum of Science and Industry
http://www.omsi.edu/

The Exploratorium
http://www.exploratorium.edu/

The Museum of Science (in Boston)
http://www.mos.org/

The Science Museum of Minnesota
http://www.ties.k12.mn.us:80/~smm/

The Miami Museum of Science
http://www.miamisci.org/

The Franklin Institute Science Museum
http://sln.fi.edu/tfi/welcome.html

THE CACTUS & SUCCULENT
PLANT MALL
Ouch!

**http://www.demon.co.uk/mace/
cacmall.html**

Here, you'll find lots of information related to the thirsty world
of cacti and succulents. And you'll find some fascinating pictures
of these interesting plants. Don't get stuck on this site too long.

ALL ABOUT FROGS
The Froggy Page

**http://www.cs.yale.edu/HTML/YALE/CS/
HyPlans/loosemore-sandra/froggy.html**

This site is full of frog pictures, images, and even frog clip art.
You can see Australian frogs, hear frog sounds and listen to
Songs of the Frog, read Froggy Tales and stories about famous
frogs. And you'll find interesting stuff on frogs that will make you
one of the foremost experts this side of the pond. Remember,
on the Internet, you can be any kind of frog you want to be!

PEOPLE, PLACES' & PURPOSE

(Eggplants, Avocados & Civilization)

DOG SLEDDING TO THE NORTH POLE
Do They Really Say Mush?

**http://www.scholastic.com/public/
Network/IAP/IAP-Home.html**

Enter the world of frozen tundra. Join the members of the
expert team of international explorers as they describe their
trek across the top of the world to the North Pole. Meet those
who took part; learn how they survived the harsh elements, what
supplies and food they needed; see the Arctic geography as they
saw it; find out all about their heroic sled dogs. This site is full
of fascinating articles and interesting photos of this historic
journey. Bundle up and visit today!

THE LIBRARY OF CONGRESS
Expired Library Card?

http://lcweb.loc.gov/homepage/lchp.html

Imagine not having to wait for that book or publication to
be returned to the stacks or that much needed research paper
to be shipped to your local library or research center. The
American Library of Congress is digitizing it's current and
future collections so that researchers can peruse the same
article simultaneously. It might still be too soon to curl up
in bed with your favorite electronic novel, but the day is close
at hand.

U.S. NATIONAL PARKS
The Beautiful and the Beasts

**http://www.gorp.com/gorp/resource/
us_national_park/main.htm**

When you stop at this site, you'll see waterfalls, geysers, rivers, and glaciers; mudpots, redwoods, canyons, and hot springs; caverns, volcanoes, and lakes; everglades and islands. With beautiful photos and facts galore, you'll have all of nature to explore. Visit the Badlands or a crater lake, the Shenandoah Mountains, or the Basin Great. Experience the beauty and magnificence of nature without the traffic or mosquitoes. This site gives you free admission to the most famous parklands in the United States (and access to many others around the world).

VIRTUAL TOURIST
Where Did I Put My Passport?

http://wings.buffalo.edu/world/vt2/

You don't need frequent flyer miles at this tourist site. And you can drink the water. Travel to, and study, some of the greatest cities in the world—without the crowds. View pictures, maps, descriptions, and official tourist guides. A whole new and brave world will open up to you and your traveling companions. And you don't have to worry about the weather or how much to tip.

NATIVEWEB
First Nation Peoples

http://web.maxwell.syr.edu/nativeweb

Here, you will get a fine glimpse of art, music, Native North American literature, events, history, and museum-related issues related to indigenous people. Come to a better understanding of a proud nation, then share your new knowledge with fellow teachers and classmates.

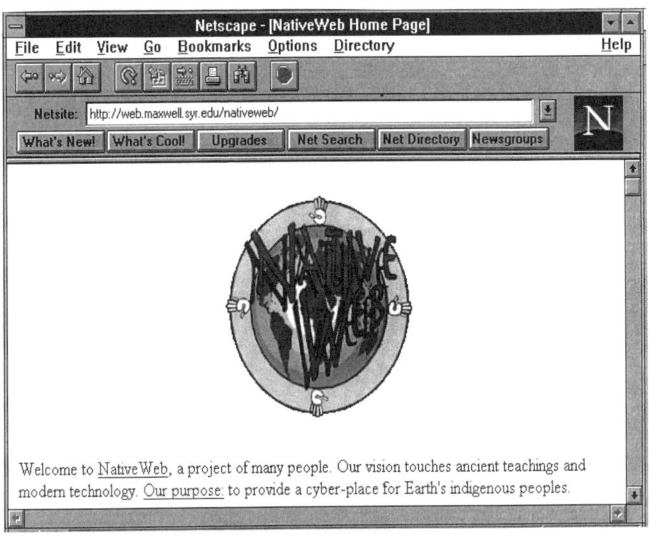

MAP VIEWER
Zoom Around the World

http://pubweb.parc.xerox.com/map

An unusual, interesting site that allows you to move here and
there, zooming in and out around the globe. At the same time,
you'll enhance your conceptual skills of space and distance.
Zoom on over and take a look.

AFRICAN ART
An Adventure to Another Continent

**http://www.lib.virginia.edu/dic/exhib/
93.ray.aa/African.html**

This exhibition presents wonderful pictures and photographs
of African art with fine descriptions. You can even engage in
interesting discussions with other visitors. Electronic art is,
without question, a unique dimension! Admission is free.

THE NETHERLANDS
An Unusual Web Site

http://www.eeb.ele.tue.nl/dhp/index.html

At this meeting point for the Netherlands (everyone is welcome),
you can connect in and about this country through a number
of clickable satellite maps. An ingenious way of serving up the
Internet for our "site-seeing" travels. You will be quite impressed
with what you learn in this small Nether Land.

VIKINGS
Welcome to Velkommen Til

**http://www.demon.co.uk/history/
index.html**

If you want to learn more about the Vikings, this site was
created with you in mind. You'll learn what life was like for
Vikings, their roles, and history. While you're here, visit the
exhibitions, museums, and archeological excavations, and
take a look at the education resources. Can anyone you know
trace his or her ancestors to northern Europe and the Vikings?

TALL SHIPS
The Sail Page

**http://www.cs.yale.edu/homes/sjl/
sail.html**

Visualize tall ships with high masts and windblown sails—the
romance and hardship intrigue youngsters and adults alike.
This is a majestic site that will link you to history, pirates,
pictures, and nautical fiction. Make sure you take a look at the
clip art. Hope to see you on deck.

THE PAINTED CAVE AT VALLON-PONT-D'ARC
Don't Write On the Walls
(You will actually be in France)

http://www.culture.fr/culture/gvpda-en.htm

Imagine turning on the lights and seeing a museum of art that no other human has seen for 20,000 years. The archeological discovery in southern France in 1994 unveiled a network of caves that holds paintings from the Paleolithic Age—horses, rhinoceros, lions, bison, wild ox, bears, panther, mammoths, and more. Much can be learned about our ancestors from these amazing discoveries.

VISIT NEW ZEALAND AND DISCOVER
What Is a Tuatara?

http://nz.com/nz/

The tuatara, the most ancient reptile, is the sole survivor of the beakheads family and lives to be over a hundred years old. At this site, you'll learn that and more about New Zealand's geography, natural history, environment, people, language, and culture. Maybe you'll even see some sheep.

SCROLLING ALONG BY THE DEAD SEA
A Walk Back in History

**http://sunsite.unc.edu/expo/
deadsea.scrolls.exhibit/intro.html**

Visit the ancient community of Qumran, where the famous Dead Sea Scrolls originated. This amazing exhibition examines how the scrolls were discovered and what they are, the people who wrote them, why they hid them, and the time period in which the people lived. Two thousand years later, a lone shepherd discovered the past.

THE VIRGINIA NEWSPAPER PROJECT
Extra! Extra!

**http://www.lib.virginia.edu/cataloging/
vnp/exhibit.html**

This site houses vintage newspaper pictures and historical articles from as early as the 1700s. It is filled with fascinating materials that will make any young historian want to read more. Great for discussion, inquiry, cooperative learning, and just plain curiosity. Aren't you glad someone saved this old stuff?

MAPMAKER, MAPMAKER, MAKE ME A MAP
Cartographer, Cartographer, Create Me a Cartograph

http://loki.ur.utk.edu/ut2kids/maps/map.html

When you land at this site, you'll find information, definitions, and terms to help you read and understand maps. If you turn left instead of right at Niagara Falls where will you be? You'll even learn about longitude and latitude (which one is which ?). We hope you can find your way to this site.

THE WORLD FACTBOOK 1995
Where in the World Is...?

http://www.odci.gov/cia/publications/95fact/index.html

When you need quick information or facts about a country, this is the place to visit. Whether you are looking for the population of El Salvador or Ethiopia, or the average life span of men in Mauritania or Mozambique, it's here. This is a rich, up-to-date resource. The tour bus leaves anytime you're ready.

THE UNDERGROUND
The Subway Navigator

http://metro.jussieu.fr:10001/bin/cities/ english

This is a great site for you and your kids to practice problem solving and put mapping skills to use. Select a starting point and a destination. At this site, you can calculate the time it takes to get there and the best route. First, using a city map, have kids pick a starting point and end point, then, using public transport, figure out the fastest route to that destination. You can go to Vienna, Mexico City, or scores of other cities from around the world. Stop here for problem solving and to learn about some of the great cities of the world, both above ground and under-ground.

PALEONTOLOGY
My Aching Back

http://sunsite.unc.edu/expo/paleo.exhibit/ paleo.html

Join a team of paleontologists (people who study life forms from the past) as they search for fossils. When you tour this site, you'll visit different geological periods, see plants and animals from long ago, learn the difference between a paleontologist and an archeologist, and a whole bunch more. Make sure you take a trip on the Web Geological Time Machine to any time and place. Pass me the fossil please.

LIVE FROM ANTARCTICA
Is It at the Top or the Bottom? Doesn't It Depend on Where I'm Standing?

http://quest.arc.nasa.gov/livefrom/livefrom.html

At this site, you'll learn about people and places near the South Pole. Read the field journals, learn about ozone holes, ask questions. This is a tremendous resource for the classroom teacher. Click on this chilly site for a bold new view of the world.

HOW TO FIND A GOOD MAP...AND KEEP IT
What Do Maps Show?

http://info.er.usgs.gov/education/teacher/what-do-maps-show/index.html

Find your way to this site and you will learn all about maps. There's lots of materials for the children; for teachers (upper elementary and junior high), there are lessons, a package you can use to teach and reinforce geographic skills required in your curriculum, a "poster" you can use as a teaching aid, and maps galore—aerial, political, road, topographical, and terrain. Mapping and map reading are powerful inquiry and problem solving tools.

CYBRARY OF THE HOLOCAUST
An Upper-Grade Experience Carefully Guided by the Teacher

http://www.best.com/~mddunn/cybrary

The Holocaust is a sensitive but critical topic for young people to study. This site is filled with facts, witness accounts, historic perspectives, and images about this dark side of world history and the severe impact it has had on civilization.

CP HEADLINES
News from a Canadian Perspective

http://xenon.xe.com/canpress/hlines.htm

Canadian News Digest provides daily summaries of news from Canada. This site also has connections to other news sites in North America.

ROUTE 66
Vrroooooooom!

http://www.cs.kuleuven.ac.be/~swa/ route66/

Route 66 has been a song, a movie, and a television show. Today people of all walks of life are retracing this piece of history that brought folks from Oklahoma to the Pacific. Read the stories, and study the maps and pictures as you take a scenic drive down this legendary superhighway now known as Historic Route 66.

THE APPALACHIAN TRAIL
Wear Heavy Socks

http://www.nando.net/AT/ATmain.html

At this site, you'll join journalists from five newspapers who hiked the 2,158-mile AppalachianTrail. Throughout, they kept journals and took photographs. From your computer, you can follow their adventures.

NATIVE AMERICAN CULTURAL RESOURCES
Fascinating Teacher or Student Resource Site

http://hanksville.phast.umass.edu/misc/ NAculture.html

An outstanding site related to Native North American culture and resources. Once here, you'll find hundreds of subsites and interesting places to visit—for example, multicultural, Tribe/ Nation, Native language, historical, and archeological. This valuable site will supplement any course about Native North Americans.

AIRSHIPS THROUGH HISTORY
Lighter Than Air

http://spot.colorado.edu/~dziadeck/airship.html

This site is a favorite of all ages. Airships, affectionately called blimps, are used by the military, for commercial aviation, and for advertising. Read all about this unusual aircraft that continues to fascinate us. Come along as we rise to the occasion and celebrate a century of airship flying.

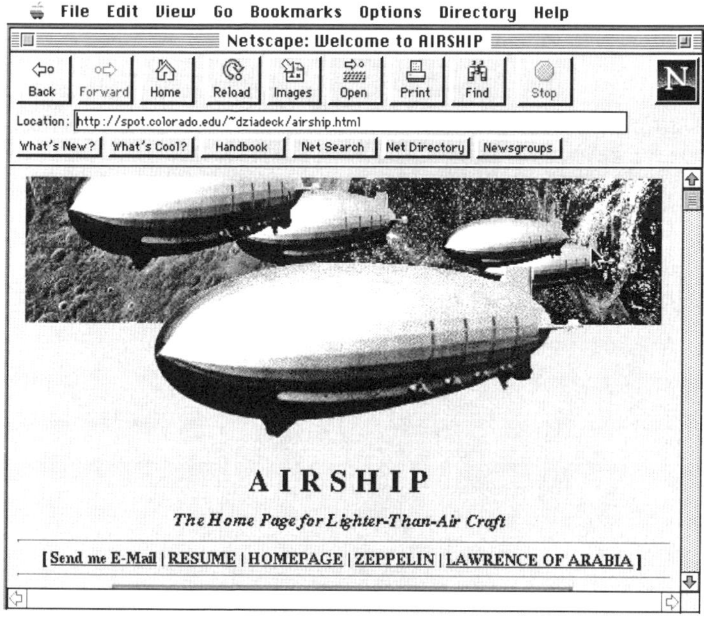

THE ANCIENT WORLD WEB
How Old Do You Feel?

**http://atlantic.evsc.virginia.edu/julia/
AncientWorld.html**

Your tour begins with Breaking News—stories about recent
discoveries that provide clues to past civilizations. Visit Africa,
Asia, Australia, Egypt, Europe, the Mediterranean, Near East, and
North and South America. Learn about ancient history through
art, archeology, history, mythology, and religion. You'll also find
connections to many other relevant sites. This is one journey
where it's okay to go backwards.

1492
The Ongoing Voyage

**http://sunsite.unc.edu/expo/1492.
exhibit/Intro.html**

This special exhibit in The Library of Congress examines the
controversial issues that surround the voyage of Christopher
Columbus and attempts to clarify the event by examining
questions related to the historical context. You can browse
through many intriguing areas of study such as What Came to
Be Called America, Conquest, Creating a New Spain in Middle
American, and Incursions into North America.

THE PIRATE PAGE
Everything You Wanted to Know About Pirates But Didn't Know Who to Ask

**http://tigger.cc.uic.edu/~toby-g/
pirates.html**

At this site, you'll learn the history of pirates on the high seas, pirate lore, differences among pirated, pirateer, and buccaneers, and see lots of images. Join us, mate, on this tour. Make sure you keep an eye on your gold.

PHOTOGRAPHS OF THE U.S. CIVIL WAR
Bring History Alive Through Primary Sources

http://rs6.loc.gov/cwphome.html

This collection contains 1,118 photographs from the American Civil War, including before and after battle scenes and portraits of both Confederate and Union officers, and enlisted men. Includes an archive and information on how to order photos. A heart-wrenching perspective of a divisive time in United States history.

MAYAQUEST EXPEDITION
The Amazing Mayans

http://mayaquest.mecc.com/

The mysteries of the ancient Mayan culture have intrigued scientists, historians, and the descendents of the Mayan for centuries. They, as well as students and teachers, continue to be fascinated by the clues that are being discovered and analyzed. At this site, you can join scientists on an expedition while they study the archeology, anthropology, flora and fauna, hieroglyphics, language, math, astronomy, politics, warfare, trade, and agriculture of these mysterious peoples. There are lots of images and interesting information to maintain interest. A rich resource for today's issues in diversity.

VIEW OF THE NILE
Egyptian Art and Archeology

http://www.memst.edu/egypt/main.html

At this site, you'll journey through the Nile Valley to ancient
Egypt (you'll actually be at the University of Memphis, Institute
of Egyptian Art and Archeology). Visit the Pyramids of King
Djoser of the Old Kingdom, and the Temple of Isis on the island
of Philae. Stroll through an exhibit of Egyptian artifacts. Brush
up on your Internet navigation and "caravan" with us on this
unusual search.

THE MAMMOTH SAGA
It's Mammoth!

**http://www.nrm.se/virtexhi/mammsaga/
mamintro.html**

An interesting exhibit about mammoths and other animals and
plants from the Ice Age. When you visit this site, located at the
Swedish Museum of Natural History, you'll learn about ecosys-
tems during the Ice Age and why many animals—for example,
the mammoth, woolly rhinoceros, saber-toothed cats (not your
basic lap variety)—became extinct.

PUEBLO INDIANS
Pueblo Cultural Center

**http://hanksville.phast.umass.edu/defs/
independent/PCC/PCC.html#toc**

A tremendous site for facts and information related to the
Pueblo Indians of the southwest United States. Includes articles
on each group of Pueblo to aid in your research, and a beautiful
mural project. A memorable and meaningful site to visit.

WHERE IS THE CABOOSE?
The Railroad

**http://www-cse.ucsd.edu/users/bowdidge/
railroad/rail-new.html**

This site includes interesting facts about trains, history of the
railroad, and great pictures. There are also links to museums,
user groups, railroad societies, and other train sites. Get on
track and you'll soon be shouting, "All aboard!"

LIGHTHOUSES
Lighthouses Over the World

http://www.noord.bart.nl/~derks/

A truly brilliant site, containing pictures/photographs of more
lighthouses than anyone knew existed. Also includes historical
facts, general information, and links to other related pages.
The lighthouse is a cultural icon. A great site for story starters,
inquiry, or simply a look at a unique collection.

CASTLES ON THE WEB
Raise the Drawbridge

http://fox.nstn.ca/~tmonk/castle/castle.html

This site is full of information and amazing pictures of the world's wondrous castles. These castles, listed in alphabetical order, show some unusual architecture and provide insight into the people who resided in and around their walls. This site is for anyone who has ever wondered who actually built the castles, where the crocodiles in the moat came from, and why the drawbridge always moaned.

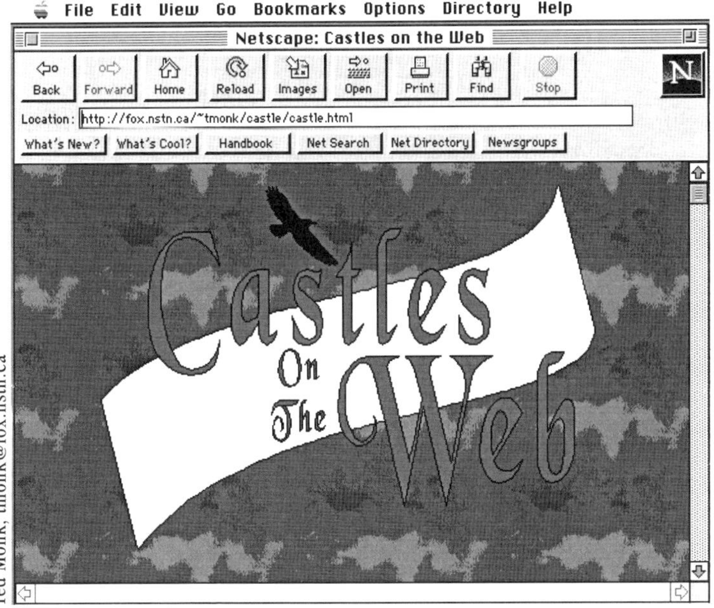

Ted Monk; tmonk@fox.nstn.ca

SAILING OVER THE DEEP BLUE SEA
The Sailing Page and Museum

**http://community.bellcore.com/mbr/
sailing-page.html#museums**

Keep your balance when you come aboard this great sea site.
You'll find information on tall ships, maritime history and
archeology, regional resources and museums, and world-wide
issues related to sailing. You'll also have links to other maritime
sites. So trim those sails and join us on this nautical voyage.

HISTORICAL COLLECTIONS FOR THE
NATIONAL DIGITAL LIBRARY
American Memory

http://rs6.loc.gov/amhome.html

Students of American history will love this site. Many documents
such as the Bill of Rights, Declaration of Independence, treaties,
personal manuscripts, and great historical photographs are
available digitally through this page. The collection is growing,
so check back periodically. Remember this site when you want
an interesting look at the past.

CNN
An address so long, you'll need to gather wood for the winter!

gopher://nysernet.org:3000/11/ Academic%20Wings/Social%20Studies/ CNN%20newsroom%20classroom%20guide

A valuable site for a variety of news and related entries (for example, science, medicine, space, people and places in the news, weather, food and health, business, technology). Includes excellent guides for the teacher and students. (Also see **http:// www.cnn.com/index.html**.)

FLAGS
Symbols Through History

http://155.187.10.12/flags/flags.html

Whether they be symbols of emerging nations or the signals from a navy vessel, flags and flag signals are a staple of organizations, large and small. Flags chronicle historical events and often reflect the changes over time. Triumphant explorers have planted flags in the frigid Arctic and in the Sea of Tranquility. Flags have flown from ocean ships to space ships, all with pride and purpose. Explore the world of flags and give us a wave.

THE GREAT BARRIER REEF
Truly a Great Wonder of the World

http://www.pi.se/~orbit/qbr.html

A trip to Australia wouldn't be complete without a visit to the Great Barrier Reef. At this site, you'll learn all about this amazing living ocean form, and the delicate balance required to maintain its presence. Stop and view this marvel of nature.

LIVELY LITERATURE

HAIKU
5-7-5

http://www.lsi.usp.br/usp/rod/poet/ haiku.html

Haiku, which originated in Japan in the thirteenth century, is a three-line verse with a 5-7-5 syllabic pattern. It is now used throughout the world as a vehicle of expression, emphasizing nature, color, season, contrast, and surprise. At this site, you'll learn to compose and understand haiku as you transcend a new dimension in writing, feeling, and expression.

CHILDREN'S LITERATURE WEB GUIDE
Books for Children & Young Adults

http://www.ucalgary.ca/~dkbrown/ index.html

Learn about upcoming conferences and book events, awards, bestsellers, movies based on books, resources for teachers and parents, and resources for writers and illustrators. Visit children's publishers and booksellers and participate in Ask the Author, a place where kids can ask their favorite author questions. This site tells you everything there is to know about children's literature on the Web.

COOL WORD OF THE DAY
Burrr...Not

http://www.dsu.edu/projects/word_of_day/word.html

This site is just what it says it is! You are given a word and definition—a great way to improve vocabulary and enjoy the art of language. You can look up past words and even submit your own. Have fun, be "cool," and enjoy this different page.

HELPING YOUR CHILD LEARN TO READ
Read Along

http://www.ed.gov/pubs/parents/Reading/index.html

We all know the value of teaching the love and appreciation of reading. This site, brought to you by the U.S. Department of Education, is full of activities for children from infancy to ten years. There are plenty of ideas and tried-and-true activities for promoting and implementing reading for young children. You'll go from the basics to read along to making books to writing. You'll also find discussions such as the place and role of parents in the school.

INDIGENOUS PEOPLES' LITERATURE
Listen and You Shall Learn

http://kuhttp.cc.ukans.edu/~marc/natlit/natlit.html

A sensitive and special site that provides literature related to and written by Indigenous peoples. Visit connected sites such as the Americas, Artists, Famous Quotes, Great Chiefs and Leaders, Indigenous Nations, Mother Earth Prayers, and much more. This site provides wonderful resources that can enhance any curriculum.

ON-LINE BOOKS
The Electronic Library

http://www.cs.cmu.edu/Web/books.html

On-line books really exist. At this site, you'll find hundreds of books and other documents on-line. Search by author, title, or use the New Book Listing. While you're here, take a look at the special exhibits. This is just the beginning of a new resource that will change how we read, what we read, and how we access our reading material. See the links that will take you to library repositories and archives from A–Z.

KID PUB
Only Lemonade Served Here

http://www.en-garde.com/kidpub/

A world where kids can publish their own stories. Kids can have their questions answered, learn about publishing, be part of collaboration, and read interesting statistics about children's stories, kid writers, and children readers. Budding authors, especially, will love this site. Point your mouse and join the fun.

AUTHOR CHAT
Ask Your Favorite Author

http://ipl.sils.umich.edu:80/youth/ AskAuthor/

At this site, part of the Internet Public Library, you can Ask the Author questions about various works and issues related to writing for children. An interesting and informative site for young and excited student authors. This is a great supplemental search to go with your literature authoring unit. Bring your questions and join in the fun.

INTERNET PUBLIC LIBRARY
No Library Card Needed Here

http://ipl.sils.umich.edu:80/

This super library has a special reference center. Click on
the picture of the desk to ask a reference question. Access
thousands of books and other interesting information. While
you're here, visit the classroom, exhibit hall, and reading room.
In this library, nobody says, "shhh" (you can even munch on
an apple!).

THE ELECTRONIC POSTCARDS
Wow, Better than French Postcards!

**http://postcards.www.media.mit.edu/
Postcards**

An amazing site. You select a postcard from those available
on the site, write a message, and send it off. The recipient is
notified by Internet e-mail that a card has been sent and can
be picked up (electronically) at the pick-up window. Have fun
and catch up on your correspondence.

WALKING IN JERUSALEM
A Site for Reading

**http://www.digimark.net/iatech/books/
waketoc.htm**

This is an on-line illustrated children's story about a child who
wakes up in the morning before his parents, and watches the
city of Jerusalem come alive.

MY BLUE SUITCASE
I'm Leaving, But I'll Be Back

**http://www.digimark.net/iatech/books/
mbstoc.htm**

A children's story dealing with the concepts of departure,
separation, and return. This site story will help us all feel better.
See the pictures and read the text as you read the tale of a
child's suitcase.

I LIVE ON A RAFT
I'm in the Mood for Poetry

**http://www.digimark.net/iatech/books/
rafttoc.htm**

Stop and read some illustrated poetry on-line: a collection of
short verses for children. Jerzy Harasymowicz, the author
of *I Live on a Raft*, is noted for his unique personal mythology
and ideas of fantasy. Children, especially, will enjoy this site.

MATH MAGIC

ASK DR. MATH
You Can Count on this Site

**http://forum.swarthmore.edu/dr.math/
dr-math.html**

If you're constantly being stumped by math problems, there
is help for you! Just ask Dr. Math. At this site you can submit
questions, and as quickly as possible, receive a reply. There is
also an index of questions and answers ranging from addition
and subtraction to square root and word problems. A great site
for both mathematically- and not-so-mathematically-inclined
students of all ages.

MATH MAGIC
Poof!

**http://www.scri.fsu.edu/~dennisl/topics/
math_magic.html**

Math *is* magic all in itself. Learn a variety of math-based "tricks"
that will stump and amaze your friends—card tricks, calculation
tricks, geometry, and topology curiosities. Impress your friends
with your "mathimagical" secrets.

COUNTING MATH
Arf, Arf, Arf

http://kao.ini.cmu.edu:5550/bdf.html

Have fun with math and let Blue Dog bark the correct answer
(you need a sound card). Kids love this site. It's weird, but cute.

MONEY, MONEY, MONEY
The Global Network Currency Converter

http://bin.gnn.com/cgi-bin/gnn/currency

This currency converter site will keep you and your kids up-to-date on the value of currency throughout the world—a great ongoing class project when dealing with global affairs. Flip a franc and convert to this site of currency.

FUN MATH
If You Say So!

http://www.uni.uiuc.edu./departments/ math/glazer/fun_math.html

Puzzles, problems, and pictures fill this site. Lots of pictures of shapes, math jokes, and other math-related ideas. We know we can count on you to visit this site.

MATHMAGIC
The Geometric Grin

http://www.npac.syr.edu/textbook/ kidsweb/math.html

Stop here for a gallery of interactive on-line geometry. Create pretty geometric pictures while learning about advanced geometry. Take a look at some fascinating color images from the Geometry Picture Archive. You'll love the mathematical magic tricks based on pure math. Great motivation for teaching and experiencing the world of mathematics.

KIDS'
FUN

LEGO
Connect to the Web With LEGO

http://legowww.homepages.com/

This site is for anyone who wants to learn more about the international phenomenon called LEGO. Just "connect and click" and you'll be offered projects, ideas, and information. You'll even get the history of LEGO bricks and the official theme song. If that isn't enough, you'll see samples of homemade constructions, games, and, yes, even robots. Snap!

THEODORE TUGBOAT
Toot! Toot!

http://www.cochran.com/TT.html

This site is for young children who want to become Theodore Tugboat's friend. The harbor community is always changing and with each change comes new adventures. Be part of the illustrated, interactive story created just for the Internet and its young site-seers. With all the fun on-line you can also download pages from the TT coloring book, so the fun continues off-line. Join Theodore for friendly, floating fun.

PUPPETS
Hi Ya Kids! Hi, Ya! Hi, Ya! Hi, Ya!
(Guess Who Said This?)

http://fox.nstn.ca/~puppets/activity.html

At this site, learn how to make puppets from the Professor.
Download patterns, performance tips, puppet ideas, and
activities galore. There's a puppeteer in each of us.

ORIGAMI
Ancient Art & Wisdom

**http://www.cs.ubc.ca/spider/jwu/
origami.html**

From A Thousand Cranes to paper airplanes, at this site you
have access to origami through the ages, images of what others
have done, and instructions on how to make your own. You'll
also find links to other origami home pages. Join the fold and
be part of this ancient and enchanting art.

THE ALPHABET
Games for Kids & Parents

http://www.klsc.com/children/Alpha.html

Reading is for everyone. Here, you'll find games that use words
and pictures, letters of the alphabet, and numbers. For children
age 3–8 years.

LITE-BRITE ON THE NET
No Outlet Required

**http://www.galcit.caltech.edu/~ta/lb/
lb.html**

At this site, you'll enjoy the new, creative art called Lite-Brite.
With Lite-Brite, children create colorful pictures by pushing
colored plastic pins into a dark piece of paper. When light from
a bulb in the back shines through the punched holes, it creates
a glowing masterpiece. Create and edit your own pictures, or
wander through the gallery. This is the "pins can't get lost"
version of the artistic entertainment center.

TIC-TAC-TOE
The Ultimate Game

http://www.bu.edu/Games/tictactoe

Originally, the game was played with three rocks and three
sticks. The "gameboard" was drawn in the sand. Two players
took turns placing a stone or stick on the board until all six
pieces were down. Then the players alternately moved their
pieces until they were all in a line. Although you'll find only the
modern version of tic-tac-toe at this site, we thought you'd like
to know how it used to be played.

GAMES FOR FUN

Pegs & Puzzles

http://www.bu.edu/htbin/pegs

Can you outwit the computer with this game of strategy?

9 Puzzle

http://www.bu.edu/Games/puzzle

A nine-piece puzzle for the child in everyone. Great fun!

SOCCER FOR KIDS
It's Worldwide

**http://www.cts.com/browse/jsent/
kidsoccer.html**

Soccer has finally caught on in North America years after it has been a successful participation and spectator sport in most of the world. It is fast, exciting, and grueling. Stop in at this site to learn more about the game and about the people who play it. Make it a goal to learn more about this fine activity.

THE JUGGLER PAGE
Don't Run Off & Join the Circus

http://www.hal.com/services/juggle/

This is an unusual site. Come in and find out about juggling
terms, services, home pages, news, festivals, and organizations;
take a look at the pictures and videos, magazines, and software.
If you don't have much time, juggle some of the things you have
to do, and visit the juggler!

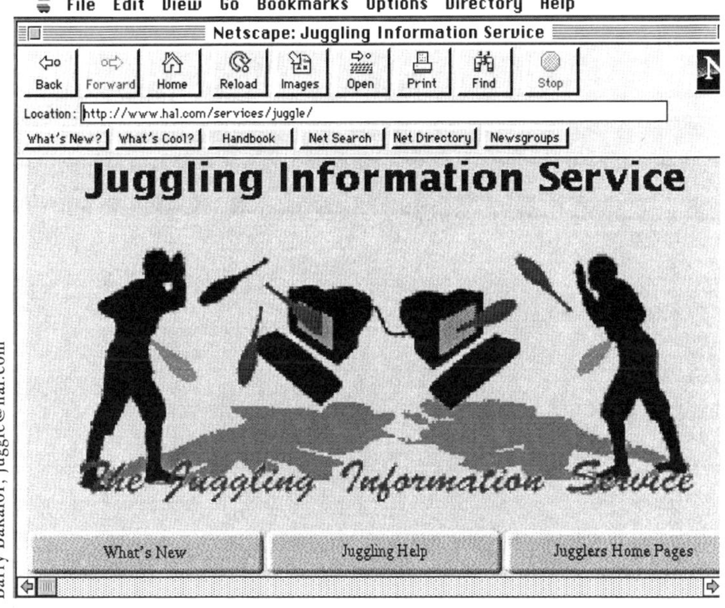

SONGS WE LOVE TO SING
On-Line Songbook

http://www.io.org/~jandd/

Here, you'll find the words to all the wonderful songs kids love
to sing. For new teachers, and teachers who know all the tunes,
this is the site to sing.

THE PEANUTS CARTOON COLLECTORS ON-LINE
Get Your Peanuts...and Snoopy Too!

http://www.dcn.davis.ca.us:80/~bang/peanuts/

Here's a brief history of Peanuts and all the gang. Learn all about
the characters who have made us laugh and "sigh" for years.
Then check out the links to other Peanuts sites. Hmm, where's
my blanket?

CYBER CYCLING
An Internet Bicycling Site

http://cyclery.com/links.html

This site is for anyone who enjoys and/or is interested in the
sport of cycling. This is the Internet bicycle resource. You'll find
lots of associations, tours, and information pages. Tighten your
helmet and peddle along with us.

"GONE FISHIN'"
The Fish Page

**http://www.inetmkt.com/fishpage/
index.html**

This site is for the angler of today and tomorrow. Catch up on what's new, peruse fishing reports from around the world, link to other fish pages, take a look at photos, and more. Drop your line or cast your Net here and you may get the catch of the day.

ANOTHER FISHIN' SITE
The Anadromous Page

**http://www.peak.org/~robertr/
fishing.html#about**

Here, you'll find recipes, resources, reports, and a photo gallery. Not to be missed!

COLOR WITH CARLOS
Color On-line with Carlos's Coloring
Book Home

http://robot0.ge.uiuc.edu/~carlosp/color/

It's simple and it's fun. Select the picture, then click and color. You'll be amazed as the colors flow from your mouse to the drawing.

YO, KERMIT!
Muppets Home Page

**http://www.ncsa.uiuc.edu/VR/BS/
Muppets/muppets.html**

Here, you'll find everything you ever wanted to know about
the muppets—from the history of the hairy guys to the Green
One himself. Join the lovable, fuzzy muppets that led millions
of kids on the road to reading and fun. You'll find general
information, episode guides, muppets on the Net, user groups,
the Semi-Official Muppet Archive, and other related on-line
sites. Everyone will have fun at this site. "Hey, Bert, where did
you put that great paper clip collection?"

CRAFTS & GAK
Play & Yack

**http://ucunix.san.uc.edu/~edavis/kids-list/
crafts/doughs.html**

At this site, you'll find some great crafts and "things"—for
example, gak (homemade silly putty), monster bubbles, and
finger paints—for the little ones. The directions are fun and
easy. Try the play dough, gak, and finger paints. Some great
recipes, too!

GAMES KIDS PLAY
You're It!

**http://www.corpcomm.net/~gnieboer/
gamehome.htm**

Games Kids Play is for everyone, not just kids. Stop here to
learn new games or find games you used to play. This is an
evolving site where readers can also be contributors. This is
a great place to visit on a rainy day.

CYBERKIDS MAGAZINE
Free On-line Magazine

**http://www.woodwind.com/mtlake/
CyberKids/index.html**

CyberKids is a great place for kids to learn and have fun.
The magazine is filled with stories and artwork created by kids,
puzzles, games, and CyberKids Interactive. You can also use
CyberKids as a launchpad to other kids' sites.

CYBER
SMORGASBORD

(AND A FEW
TASTY LINKS)

THE KITE SITE
String Me Along

**http://www.latrobe.edu.au/Glenn/KiteSite/
Kites.html**

This site is for kite enthusiasts—young and old. Over the years, kites have provided both models of aerodynamics and endless hours of entertainment and dreams. Everyone loves the thrill of flying a kite. Kites are created and exhibited as art and science. Take a look at some of the magnificent kites while you're here. Check out some of the festivals held world-wide. Try links to other kite sites or browse through the users group. Then have fun making your own at home or as a class project. Hold onto your hat and grab your kite. Join us while we fly to new adventures on the Internet.

MERRY-GO-ROUND
My First Horse Only Went in Circles

**http://www.access.digex.net/~rburgess/
nca.html**

When you climbed up into the saddle, you just knew the ride would be exciting. You placed your feet in the stirrups, shouted "giddy-up," and soon could hear the music in your ears and feel the wind upon your face. Up and down and all around you went on your trusted horse…Everyone loves the merry-go-round. Now you can read about some of the first carousels, view fantasy carousel art, visit the New England Carousel Museum, and more. At this site, you'll go in circles!

ROLLER COASTER COMPENDIUM
The World of Roller Coasters

http://sunsite.unc.edu/darlene/coaster/coaster.html

If you're a roller coaster thrill seeker, this site is for you. Learn the facts, names, locations, and designers. There's enough information here for you to plan your next summer vacation around the best roller coasters in the United States. Raise your arms above your head, and with your nose type in the address of this heart-pounding, white-knuckle Internet site. When the fun is over, pick us up by the snack bar.

ANIMATION PAGE
Toon-In

http://www.disney.com/

From movie talk to coloring books, it's all at this site featuring the Disney animation favorites. You can connect to legendary adventures through animation and movies. Be sure to be here when the new features are presented and discussed. Visit MoviePlex and International MoviePlex. Fun for kids and adults of all ages.

@ BAT
Take Me Out to the Ball Game

http://www2.pcy.mci.net/mlb/index.html

Major League Baseball steals home with this action-packed
Web site. Includes information on the leagues, scores and stats,
News and Notes, Photo Gallery, and more. You'll be able to follow
all the teams, league standings, today's games, and yesterday's
results. Swing over to this site today. It's a home run!

THE CANDID VOYEUR
Click!

**http://www.eskimo.com/~irving/
web-voyeur/**

You can see the world from actual camera pictures being
taken every few minutes. This site is strange, but gives
interesting views of places like Pikes Peak Colorado and San
Francisco Bay. Sneak a peak at the Hollywood sign in California,
Buckman Elementary School in Oregon, the University of
Western Australia, even the Netherlands. The sequencing, time,
change, and even the weather make this a site with many
applications to the curriculum.

LOONEY TUNES
"What's Up, Doc?"

**http://www.usyd.edu.au/~swishart/
looney.html**

Here, some of your favorite cartoons come alive in sight and sound. Visit Bugs Bunny, Daffy Duck, Pepe Le Pew, Taz, Yosemite Sam, Sylvester, Tweety Bird, and lots of others. You can have great fun imitating, drawing, or writing about these characters. You'll probably feel just a bit looney when you leave.

FROM TIME WARNER
Pathfinder

http://www.pathfinder.com
(go to Just for Kids)

At this multi-use site, students can click on Just For Kids to find "kidstuff," Time For Kids, and *Sports Illustrated for Kids.* For the teacher, try *Time, Life, People,* or *Money* magazine. For a quick look at the day's news, check out Today's Headlines. A great site for keeping in touch. Be a pathfinder on the Internet. Others will follow.

TOFU FOR YOU
One Click on the Vegetarian Site

http://www.fatfree.com/recipes/tofu/

Tofu can be prepared in a variety of ways and is a tasty and healthy alternative to meat. This is your chance to discover what you can do with tofu (other than float it in soup). Try tofu nuggets, eggplant and tofu, tofu-kabob, tofu loaf, and other interesting recipes. If we are changing the way we learn, why not change the way we eat?

WE CAN MEET ALL YOUR "VEGGIE" NEEDS
The Vegetarian Pages

http://catless.ncl.ac.uk/Vegetarian

A great page for a new way of thinking, eating, living, and staying fit. Or maybe you just like eating vegetables. This site has information on nutritional, health-related issues, and you'll find lots of recipes. You'll also find links to many other vegetarian sites.

VEGETABLES AGAIN!
Everyone Loves Them

http://envirolink.org/arrs/VRG/home.html

At this site, you'll find information about vegetarian lifestyles and lots of recipes. Don't be afraid to explore and experiment as you read.

BRIDGES
Life's Crossings

**http://william-king.www.drexel.edu/top/
bridge/CBbyC.html**

This site pays tribute to why the bridge is there and what it means to bridge. It contains wonderful information about covered bridges, with accompanying photos that are perfect for story starters or simply gazing at. Make sure you cross a bridge on your tour of the Internet.

VIRTUAL STAMP COLLECTING
Lick, Lick, Lick!

**http://www.stampworld.com/sites/
stmpvlib.html**

Stamps have become an artful chronicle of the modern world. At this extraordinary site filled with people, places, and events, you'll find stamps from Elvis to Ethiopia. A network of dedicated philatelists (put that on your weekly spelling list) from around the world keep this site going.

CALVIN & HOBBES
Home Page & Picture Archive

**http://www.eng.hawaii.edu/Contribs/ju/
Index.html**

Enjoy the antics of Calvin and Hobbes as they make their way in Cyberspace. View hilarious comic strips and single panels.

COOKING OVER THE CAMPFIRE
The Virtual Campsite Cookbook

**http://skypoint.com/members/srtobin/
recipes/recipes.html**

Stop at this cook site for a taste of good camping food. You'll
find easy-to-cook recipes that are perfect for kids to make and
great for camping trips. It's all right here, from trail mix to
crawfish. Of course, there's S'mores and hot dogs, too. This
essential site will make your meals so good, you'll forget you're
homesick.

THE COFFEE SITE
Cup of "J" in the Morning

**http://astro.ocis.temple.edu/~ghinkle/
java.html**

This site has links to hundreds of coffee spots that will tell you
everything there is to know about coffee—and more. So kick
back, enjoy one last cup before the day begins, and do a little
daydreaming.

CHOCOLATE, CHOCOLATE, CHOCOLATE
Food for the Soul

**http://www.godiva.com/resources/
index.html**

Many ancient cultures understood the special relationship between cocoa and the human spirit. At this luscious site, learn the history, terminology, facts, and trivia about the world of chocolate. You can also connect to other chocolate sites.

PERFECT PIZZA & PASTA
The Recipe Archive Index

**http://www.honors.indiana.edu/~veggie/
recipes.cgi/categories.html**

Here, you'll find a cookbook that includes appetizers, cookies, ethnic dishes, soups and vegetable recipes, even crockpot delicacies. There's something to tantalize every palate, discriminating or not. A great site for kids and adults.

SOUPS ON!
Bean, Borscht & Beef

**http://www.vuw.ac.nz/who/Amy.Gale/
recipes/soup/index.html**

More great recipes from those Cyber cooks Amy and Gale. You'll find hundreds of soups—hearty soups to warm you on a chilly day, lentil soup that'll take you to the shores of the Mediterranean, chicken soup to cure whatever ails you, and more.

ROUGH RUGBY
International Rugby League

http://www.brad.ac.uk/~cgrussel/

Rugby is fast becoming a popular sport throughout the world. It's rough, wild, and not for the timid. Visit this site for information on everything a rugby fan needs to know.

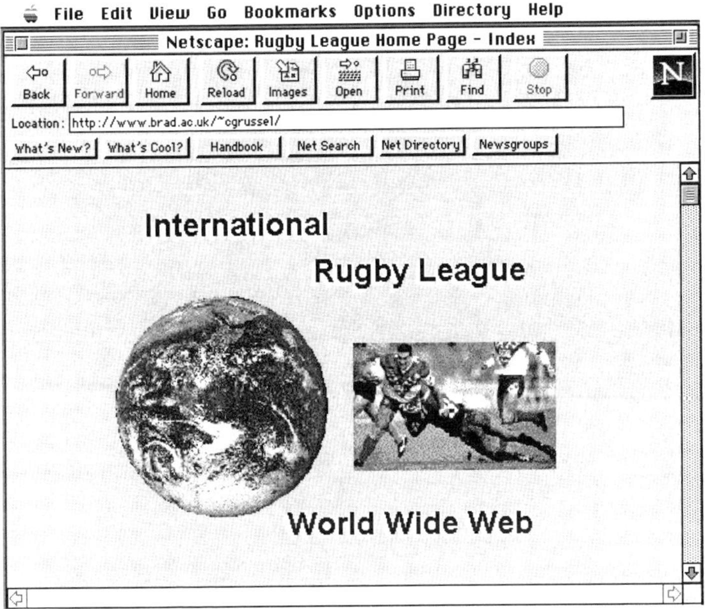

THE SNOW PAGE
Do You Ski? (Teacher Winter Break Site)

**http://rmd-www.mr.ic.ac.uk/snow/
snowpage.html**

If you're thinking about a skiing vacation in the mountains, then
this may be the site for you. You'll also find information on snow
boarding and resorts, trail maps and user groups, magazines and
travel services. Watch out for the moguls!

PROFESSIONAL HOCKEY
On the Ice

**http://maxwell.uhh.hawaii.edu/hockey/
hockey.html**

Make no mistake on these razor-sharp skates. Click on this site to
slide into the exciting and fast-moving world of ice hockey. From
regular season standings to the Stanley Cup playoffs, get the latest
information about your favorite teams and players.

THE ROLLERBLADE PAGE
Skate the Net

**http://anansi.panix.com:80/userdirs/rbs/
Skate/**

At this site, you'll find out what's new in rollerblading, clubs,
organizations, and products. It includes articles on people,
rollerhockey, speedskating, technical stuff, and where to skate.
Of course, you'll find fine photos as well. Put your polyurethane
to the pavement. Don't forget to wear your pads and helmet.

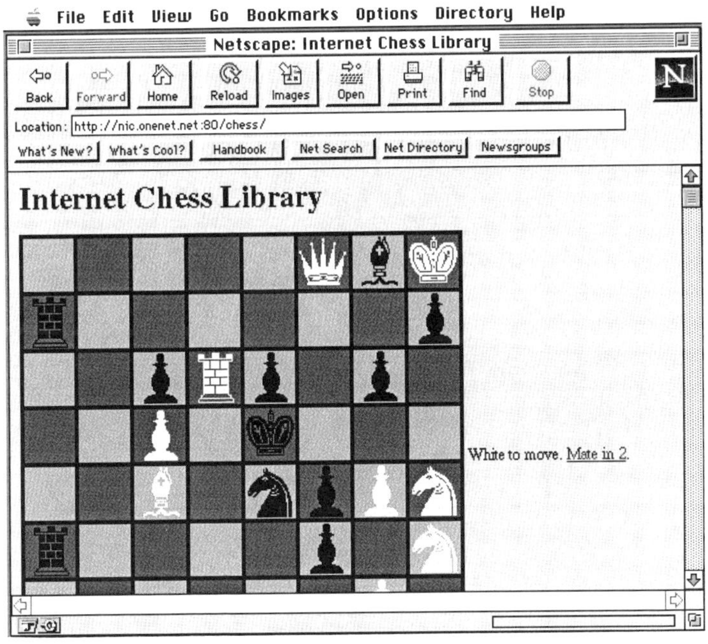

CHESS FOR EVERYONE
Kings, Queens & Knights

http://nic.onenet.net:80/chess/

A fine site for the discriminating chess enthusiast. Play this game
of strategy and decision making in the classroom or at home on
a rainy day. Hold an on-line, ongoing chess tournament.

HORSE & RODEO
It's a Stampede

**http://www.interealm.com/p/ratzloff/
horse.htm**

A great site for horse enthusiasts or anyone who wants a taste
of western life. You'll find lots of information on rodeos and
horses, and links to other related sites. Rope and tie this site
for a great outdoor experience.

STAR TREK
The Final Frontier

http://198.147.111.30/~werdna/sttng/

If you're a Trekkie, this site is for you—it's full of great
pictures and stories of the characters from StarTrek: T.N.G.
Enjoy this interplanetary site, and we hope you find your way
safely in (Cyber) space.

THE MAGIC MENU
Magic Guide to the Web

**http://www.uelectric.com/
allmagicguide.html**

A truly magical place where magicians meet. Step into The
Magic Castle where magicians share their illusions and trick-
ery. Fun for everyone. Hey, what happened to my computer?
It was just here!

DANCING BY
The Dance Page

http://www.ens-lyon.fr/~esouche/danse/ dance.html

At this site, the world of dance comes alive. The great dance companies of the world share their stories. Visit the National Ballet of Canada, the New York City Ballet, and others. See wonderful drawings, paintings, and pictures of dancers. A rich and enduring site for those interested in the art and love of the dance. Step softly to this site.

KIDS' LINKS

GENERAL MULTIPLE SITES FOR KIDS

The following sites contain some wonderful places for kids. When you arrive at the main site, you may have to click on the "links" to move to the site of choice. By going forward and back, you will get almost everywhere you dream of (that would be nice).

KIDS ONLY!
The Milwaukee Web

http://www.execpc.com/milwaukee/kids/

This site is dedicated entirely to kids on the Internet. It is a place to explore, have fun, and learn. Enjoy on-line coloring books, anagrams, and the kid's bulletin board. Don't forget Mr. Telephoneman, Snacktime, and Sports.

KIDS WEB-WORLD WIDE WEB
Digital Library for SchoolKids

http://www.npac.syr.edu/textbook/kidsweb/

This general site offers a smorgasbord of subsites for children. This is the "Yellow Brick Road" of Web sites. Step up to art, drama, literature, music, astronomy, biological and life sciences, chemistry, computers, environmental science, math, weather, geography, sports, the reference desk, and games.

BERIT'S BEST SITES FOR CHILDREN

**http://www.cochran.com/theosite/
ksites.html**

This is another of those multiple-side "indexes" that lists interesting sites for kids. These lists are worth the visit for those of you who want to see what's there and pick what you want. You may also find sites you've visited before. That's what "linking" and "webbing" are all about. You'll find sites directing you to art, animals, astronomy, dinosaurs, earth, elementary schools, families, frogs, history, science, sharks, stories, and much more. This type of site is updated on a regular basis.

EXPLORE!

Kids On Campus

**http://www.tc.cornell.edu/Kids.on.Campus/
KOC94/koc94home.html**

This site includes links to libraries, dinosaurs, weather, movies, and even information on the solar system.

Classroom Connect

**http://www.wentworth.com/classroom/
newedu.htm**

This site is kind of like a "grab bag." Come on in and see what you get. It's fun and informative. New every month.

Kidding Around

**http://alexia.lis.uiuc.edu/~watts/
kiddin.html**

This site is a place where middle school kids and teenagers can
hang out.

Kids' Corner

http://www.ot.com/kids/

Here, you'll find puzzles, games, interactive stories, and links to
other sites.

Canadian Kids Page

**http://www.onramp.ca/~lowens/
107kids.htm**

This site contains great Canadian pages, activities, and links to
other kids' pages and sites.

The Kids On the Web

http://www.zen.org/~brendan/kids.html

Here, you'll find games, coloring pages, and links to other sites.

Kids.Com

http://kids.com.

At this site, you'll find kids' home pages, organizations, and
links to other sites.

REFERENCES, RESOURCES & REALITY

HOTLIST OF K–12 INTERNET SCHOOL SITES
Kids On Line

**http://toons.cc.ndsu.nodak.edu/
~sackmann/k12.html**

Here, you'll find a list of schools that are on the Internet. Drop in for a visit and find out what others are doing. From the momentous to the mundane, join your fellow students and colleagues for a stroll along the Web Highway.

U.S. DEPARTMENT OF EDUCATION
Equal Access to Education

http://www.ed.gov/index.html

This site provides straightforward information to American educators, and policy makers and parents interested in educational issues. Sign on for the National Education Goals, Teacher's Guide to the Department of Education, Researchers' Guide to the U.S. Department of Education, Goals for the Year 2000, U.S. Department of Education's Main Gopher Server, Newsletters, Press Releases, Recent Publications and other educational resources. This is the professional's resource guide to education. It's not exactly the teacher's room, but who knows who you'll meet.

U.S. FEDERAL GOVERNMENT ON THE INTERNET
Friends, Fun & Frolics

http://www.fie.com/www/us_gov.htm

Check out this site to find out what the United States government
is up to. Some of the offices you can access are

Office of the President
Federal Information Exchange
Commerce Department
Office of the Vice President
Department of Agriculture
National Oceanic and Atmospheric Administration
Economic Development Administration
Bureau of the Census
Climate Prediction Center
National Marine Fisheries
National Patent and Trademark Office
Office of the Secretary of the Defense
Joint Chiefs of Staff
Department of Energy
Department of Education
Department of Science Education and Technical Information
Department of the Interior
Johnson Space Center
NASA On-line Information

CANADA ON THE INTERNET
The True North

**http://unixg.ubc.ca:7001/0/providers/hss/
zil/poli/canpoli/canpol2.html**

This site links you to federal and provincial government
agencies, politics, the media, statistical information, Native
studies, law, electronic journals, and more.

VIRTUAL SHAREWARE LIBRARY
Teacher Resource Site

**http://www.acs.oakland.edu/cgi-bin/
vsl-front**

This site catalogues about 110,000 files with a search engine
(search index), enabling you to search for whatever you want.
Learn about shareware on this site—download the software,
try it out, and if you like it, pay a nominal fee. If you don't pay,
your computer won't self-destruct, but you'll need to do a
karma check.

AskERIC
Eric, Where Are You?

http://ericir.syr.edu/

ERIC (Educational Resources Information Center) is a national
information system supported by the U.S. Department of
Education. You'll find lesson plans, databases, collections,
the AskERIC virtual library, and much more. Perfect for
research or gaining information related to educational issues.

ALL ABOUT APPLES, MACS, AND OTHER LINKS
Apples, Apples Everywhere

http://www.netins.net/showcase/ macintosh/

This source is an important site for teachers, parents, and kids
who want to find out more about the world of Apple computers.
It includes the Apple Computer Home Page, information on
equipment prices, software catalog, Mac archives, *MacUser
Magazine,* as well as dozens and dozens of interesting and
useful links.

COMPUTER-USING EDUCATORS
What's a CUE?

http://www.cue.org/

CUE (Computer-Using Educators), is the oldest and largest
organization in the United States dedicated to learning, teaching,
and technology. CUE is a nonprofit educational corporation
providing networking and resources for educators, related
to computer technology and education. Check out this
important site.

AREAS & ZIPS
The Reference Page

**http://www.infomall.org/kidsweb/
reference.html**

This is the site to go to when you're looking for information
like zip codes, area codes, libraries on the Internet, Roget's
Thesaurus, Biographical Directory, American English Dictionary,
Acronym Dictionary, and much more.

WEBSTER'S DICTIONARY
What Does It Mean?

http://civil.colorado.edu/htbin/dictionary

A great site for kids to practice the power of the electronic
resources. To find out definitions and the correct spelling of
a word, simply enter the word in the Search box and click.

AMERICAN UNIVERSITIES
A Higher Site

**http://www.clas.ufl.edu/CLAS/
american-universities.html**

At this site, you can connect to American universities and find
out information on a wide variety of subject areas. Or you can
have your classes connect to a university class of perspective
teachers or microbiologists. This site also includes links to
Canadian and international universities.

COLLEGES AND UNIVERSITIES AROUND THE WORLD
Planet Earth

http://www.nosc.mil/planet_earth/uni.html

This is another site you can use to go to universities and
colleges all around the globe. In seconds—literally—you can
connect with colleagues or "new" friends in the Netherlands
or Iceland, Auckland or Singapore. This is a tremendous way
to "site-see" the education world from the classroom or home.
Great potential for linkages with school classrooms and
international universities. Set your "sites" on higher education.

VISIT MY SCHOOL
Classroom Connect Classroom Web on the Net

http://ns.wentworth.com:80/classweb/

This is a great site to post your school's home page and visit schools in Australia, Canada, Japan, Mexico, New Zealand, Sweden, and the United States. Chalk one up for your classroom!

MEDIA ON THE WEB
Television, Newspapers & Periodicals

http://www.well.com/news.html

Check out this site for a new way of thinking about the information that reaches us. Newspapers, magazines, and television guides no longer need to be delivered to the door. Just click on this media site and send your mouse to pick up the latest edition. (Give the pooch a break today!)

NOTES

NOTES

NOTES

Also by Gary Garfield and Suzanne McDonough

"Sound classroom ideas that encourage students to write, share and gather information via telecommunications..
—Pamela Korporaal, President of CUE (Computer-Using Educators)

Telecommunications is fast becoming an essential tool in the classroom—it offers teachers and students infinite sources of information and knowledge. In *Modems, Megabytes & Me!* you'll see just how easy and inexpensive it is to integrate telecommunications into your school curriculum. You'll find:

- suggestions on how to set up workstations
- advice on how to go on-line and connect to partnership schools
- dozens of practical ideas and fun activities
- a review of basic computer terms and computing procedures, and much more

Now is the time to introduce your kids to this "new" way of learning, problem solving, and decision making.

ISBN 1-895411-78-5 $16

TO ORDER OR FOR MORE INFORMATION

WRITE
Peguis Publishers
100-318 McDermot Avenue
Winnipeg, Manitoba
Canada R3A OA2

CALL TOLL FREE
1-800-667-9673

OR SEND US A FAX
1-204-947-0080